Piano

Classical
Piano Anthology 1

30 Original Works
Including pieces by Mozart, Beethoven, Hummel and Weber

ED 13234
ISMN M-2201-3104-2
ISBN 978-1-84761-144-4

www.schott-music.com

Mainz • London • Berlin • Madrid • New York • Paris • Prague • Tokyo • Toronto
© 2010 SCHOTT MUSIC Ltd, London • Printed in Germany

Acknowledgements / Remerciements / Danksagung

I am grateful to Mary and David Bowerman whose generous support has enabled the CD to be recorded in the excellent setting of Champs Hill Music Room. A special mention must go to the production team of the CD, Ateş Orga and Ken Blair, for their expertise and contribution to this project.

Je remercie Mary et David Bowerman dont le généreux soutien a permis d'enregistrer le CD dans les excellentes conditions offertes par le Champs Hill Music Room. Il me faut également citer tout particulièrement l'équipe de production du CD, Ateş Orga et Ken Blair, pour leur savoir-faire et leur précieuse contribution à ce projet.

Ich danke Mary und David Bowerman für ihre großzügige Unterstützung, die es ermöglicht hat, die CD im großartigen Ambiente des Champs Hill Music Room aufzunehmen. Ein besonderer Dank geht an das Produktionsteam der CD, Ateş Orga und Ken Blair für ihr Know-how und ihren Beitrag zu diesem Projekt.

Nils Franke

ED 13234
British Library Cataloguing-in-Publication Data.
A catalogue record for this book is available from the British Library
ISMN M-2201-3104-2
ISBN 978-1-84761-144-4

CD recorded in Champs Hill, West Sussex, 8th June 2010, on a Steinway D Concert Grand with Nils Franke, Piano
Producer: Ateş Orga
Editor and Engineer: Ken Blair
Cover design: H.-J. Kropp
Cover image: 'Wasserfall bei Tivoli' (1800-1810), by Johann Martin von Rohden (b. 30th July 1778 in Kassel; d. 9th September 1868 in Rome)

French translation: Michaëla Rubi
German translation: Heike Brühl
Music setting and page layout: Darius Heise-Krzyszton, www.notensatzstudio.de

Printed in Germany S&Co.8548

Contents / Sommaire / Inhalt

The Pieces / Les pièces / Die Stücke

Introduction

The present collection of piano pieces is the first volume in a series of four books covering piano music in the classical period from grades 1–8. It follows on from a format established in the Romantic Piano Anthologies Vols. 1–4 (ED 12912 to ED 12915).

While anthologies are, inevitably, a personal selection of music they can nevertheless be underpinned by specific selection criteria. In the case of the present series, it has been my intention to include works that are idiomatically written, are indicative of their period and, above all, are useful in the development of pianistic skills for players at this stage of their development.

In the selection of repertoire I have tried to achieve a balance between established teaching pieces, rare works of the period, and between some of the main composers of the era and their lesser-known contemporaries. I hope that this can in some way attempt to reflect the diversity of styles within music from the 1760s to circa 1820. After this selection had been made, some interesting connections began to emerge, some of which reflect the work circumstances of composer-musicians of that time: geographical locations for musical activity and patterns for concert tours. Much of the music in this volume has an Austrian connection: Haydn, both Mozarts, Beethoven, Schubert and the entrepreneurial publisher-composers Diabelli and Haslinger. There are the touring virtuosi Haessler, Steibelt, Hummel, Weber and those performers who made a particular city their home, for example Hässler and Steibelt in St. Petersburg, and Cramer in London.

Each anthology contains a few pieces that are deliberate, yet manageable challenges to the piano student, either in terms of musical complexity or technical requirements. In this volume, pieces 25 and 28 may fall within that category. The repertoire is presented broadly in an order of ascending difficulty though I hope that the suggested sequence can be seen as a recommendation, rather than a restriction. The music included in this book is aimed at players of Grade 1–2 standard (UK) or late beginner to elementary (USA), or pianists of two or more years' playing experience (Europe).

The teaching notes are designed to assist students by offering some suggestions on how to approach a particular section within a piece. Also included are suggestions for topics that may need to be considered when playing classical piano music on a modern instrument, as the fortepiano of the late 18th century was of a different construction to the modern piano. The commentary cannot, and is not intended to, replace the collaborative spirit of exploration that teachers and students share in their lessons.

One of the most rewarding aspects of instrumental teaching is watching students become independent learners who make their own decisions and develop their own performance skills. I hope that the Classical Piano Anthologies can in some way contribute to this development.

Nils Franke

Introduction

Ce recueil de pièces pour piano constitue le premier volet d'une collection en quatre volumes couvrant le répertoire pour piano de la période classique, du niveau 1 au niveau 8. Du point de vue formel, il se calque sur le format établi dans l'Anthologie du piano romantique, volumes 1 à 4 (ED 12912 to ED 12915).

Le fait qu'une anthologie reflète inévitablement des choix personnels n'empêche pas qu'elle puisse néanmoins être sous-tendue pas des critères de sélection spécifiques. Pour ce qui concerne la présente collection, j'ai choisi d'inclure des œuvres à l'écriture idiomatique, caractéristiques de leur période et, avant tout, utiles au développement des compétences pianistiques des instrumentistes à ce niveau de leur progression.

Pour ce qui concerne le choix du répertoire, j'ai tenté de réaliser un équilibre aussi bien entre des pièces appartenant traditionnellement au répertoire pédagogique et des œuvres rares de cette période, qu'entre des compositeurs majeurs et leurs contemporains moins célèbres. J'espère que cela permettra en quelque sorte d'illustrer la diversité des styles musicaux des années 1760 à 1820 environ. Des connexions intéressantes ont commencé à émerger à l'issue de cette sélection, dont certaines reflètent les conditions de travail des musiciens-compositeurs de ce temps : les lieux géographiques de l'activité musicale et le fonctionnement des tournées de concerts. Une grande part des musiques contenues dans ce recueil présente des liens avec l'Autriche : Haydn, les deux Mozart, Beethoven, Schubert ainsi que les deux éditeurs-compositeurs Diabelli et Haslinger. Certains virtuoses comme Haessler, Steibelt, Hummel et Weber voyageaient beaucoup dans le cadre de longues tournées tandis que d'autres s'établissaient dans une ville en particulier, par exemple Hässler et Steibelt à Saint-Pétersbourg ou Cramer à Londres.

Chaque anthologie propose volontairement quelques pièces constituant un défi délibéré, mais toujours surmontable, pour l'élève pianiste, que soit en termes de complexité musicale ou d'exigences techniques. Dans ce volume par exemple, les pièces 25 et 28 peuvent entrer dans cette catégorie. Le répertoire est présenté globalement par ordre croissant de difficulté, mais j'espère que la progression suggérée sera considérée davantage comme une suggestion que comme une contrainte. La musique proposée dans cet ouvrage s'adresse à des musiciens de niveau 1 à 2 standard (RU) ou débutant à élémentaire (USA), ou à des pianistes possédant au moins deux années de pratique instrumentale (Europe).

Les notes pédagogiques ont pour objectif d'aider les élèves en leur suggérant des axes de travail pour l'approche de certains passages spécifiques à l'intérieur des morceaux. Dans la mesure où le pianoforte de la fin du 18e siècle était de facture différente du piano moderne, elles proposent également des réflexions sur les thématiques à aborder lorsque l'on joue de la musique classique sur un instrument moderne. Ces commentaires ne peuvent ni ne prétendent se substituer à l'esprit de collaboration et d'exploration que partagent le maître et l'élève pendant la leçon.

L'un des aspects les plus gratifiants de l'enseignement instrumental est de voir ses élèves devenir indépendants, expérimenter différentes pistes musicales et développer leurs propres dons. J'espère qu'à leur manière, ces Anthologies du piano classique pourront contribuer à ce développement.

Nils Franke

Einleitung

Die vorliegende Sammlung ist der erste Band einer vierbändigen Reihe mit klassischer Klaviermusik für alle Schwierigkeitsgrade. Sie ist genauso aufgebaut wie die Romantic Piano Anthology Bd. 1–4 (ED 12912 bis ED 12915).

Eine Anthologie stellt zwar immer eine subjektive Auswahl von Musikstücken dar, doch können natürlich bestimmte Auswahlkriterien herangezogen werden. Mein Anliegen bei der Zusammenstellung der vorliegenden Reihe war eine Auswahl von Musikstücken, die idiomatisch geschrieben, typisch für ihre Epoche und vor allem im Hinblick auf klavierspielerische Aspekte für Pianisten dieser Spielstufe nützlich sind.

Bei der Auswahl der Stücke habe ich versucht, ein ausgewogenes Verhältnis zwischen bewährtem Unterrichtsmaterial und seltener gespielten klassischen Werken sowie zwischen einigen der wichtigsten Komponisten dieser Epoche und ihren weniger bekannten Zeitgenossen herzustellen. Ich hoffe, dass dies die Stilvielfalt der Musik von ca. 1760 bis 1820 widerspiegelt. Nachdem die Auswahl der Stücke getroffen war, ergaben sich einige interessante Zusammenhänge in Bezug auf die Gegebenheiten der Komponisten und Musiker jener Zeit: die geografische Lage der musikalischen Aktivitäten sowie bestimmte Muster hinsichtlich der Konzertreisen. Viele Musikstücke in diesem Band haben einen Bezug zu Österreich: Haydn, beide Mozarts, Beethoven, Schubert und die Verleger und Komponisten Diabelli und Haslinger. Da sind die Tournee-Virtuosen Häßler, Steibelt, Hummel und Weber sowie die Musiker, die in einer bestimmten Stadt heimisch wurden wie z. B. Häßler und Steibelt in St. Petersburg und Cramer in London.

Jede Anthologie enthält einige Stücke, die entweder wegen ihrer musikalischen Komplexität oder wegen ihrer technischen Anforderungen eine bewusste, jedoch zu bewältigende Herausforderung für die Klavierschüler darstellen. In diesem Band gehören die Stücke 25 und 28 dazu. Die Stücke sind weitgehend nach aufsteigendem Schwierigkeitsgrad geordnet, wobei die vorgeschlagene Reihenfolge als Empfehlung und nicht als Einschränkung aufgefasst werden sollte. Die Stücke in diesem Buch richten sich an Spieler der Stufe 1–2 (Großbritannien), Anfänger mit Vorkenntnissen (USA) bzw. Pianisten mit mindestens zwei Jahren Spielpraxis (Europa).

Die Spielhinweise sollen die Schüler mit Hilfe von Vorschlägen für bestimmte Passagen an das jeweilige Stück heranführen. Darüber hinaus enthält die Anthologie Vorschläge, die eventuell berücksichtigt werden müssen, wenn man klassische Klaviermusik auf einem modernen Instrument spielt, da sich das Pianoforte des späten 18. Jahrhunderts vom modernen Klavier unterschied. Die Anmerkungen können und sollen jedoch nicht die gemeinsame Beschäftigung von Lehrern und Schülern mit dem Stück im Unterricht ersetzen.

Eine der schönsten Belohnungen beim Unterrichten eines Instruments ist, zu beobachten, wie die Schüler unabhängig werden, eigene Entscheidungen treffen und ihren eigenen Spielstil entwickeln. Ich hoffe, dass die Classical Piano Anthology einen Betrag zu dieser Entwicklung leisten kann.

Nils Franke

1. Minuet in D Minor

Leopold Mozart
(1719–1787)

(♩ = 144–152)

Fine

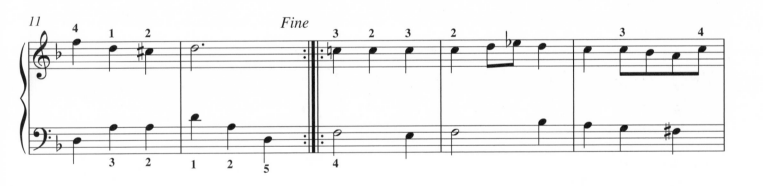

D.C. al Fine

© 2010 Schott Music Ltd, London

2. Minuet in F Major

Leopold Mozart
(1719–1787)

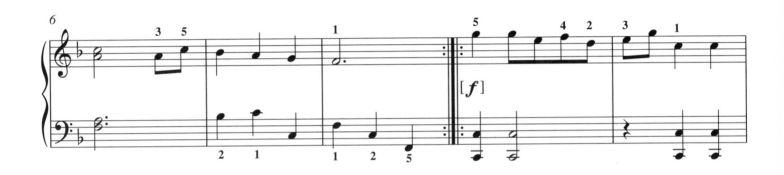

una corda

3. Minuet

KV6/IIIa

Wolfgang Amadeus Mozart
(1756–1791)

• aus / from / de: L. Mozart, Notenbuch für Nannerl / Notebook for Nannerl, Schott ED 9006

4. Piano Piece

Op. 125 No. 7

Anton Diabelli
(1781–1858)

5. Piano Piece
Op. 125 No. 6

Anton Diabelli
(1781–1858)

6. Minuet
KV1e

Wolfgang Amadeus Mozart
(1756–1791)

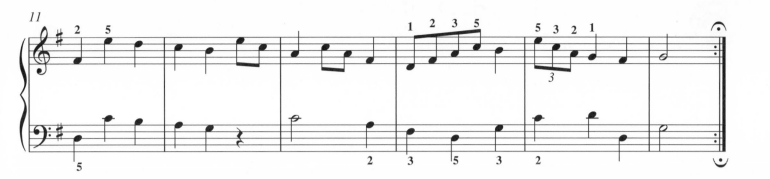

7. Minuet in C Major

Leopold Mozart
(1719–1787)

(♩ = 132–136)

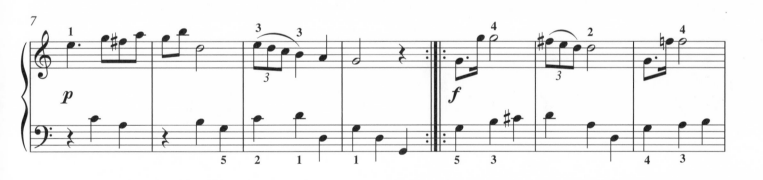

• from / de / aus: L. Mozart, Notenbuch für Nannerl / Notebook for Nannerl, Schott ED 9006

8. Deutscher Tanz

Hob. IX: 8

Joseph Haydn
(1732–1809)

9. Ecossaise

Op. 52 No. 5

Johann Nepomuk Hummel
(1778–1837)

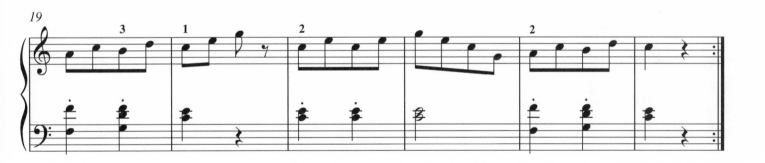

10. Sonatina in C Major

Allegro non troppo ($\frac{1}{2}$ = 108–116)

Tobias Haslinger
(1787–1842)

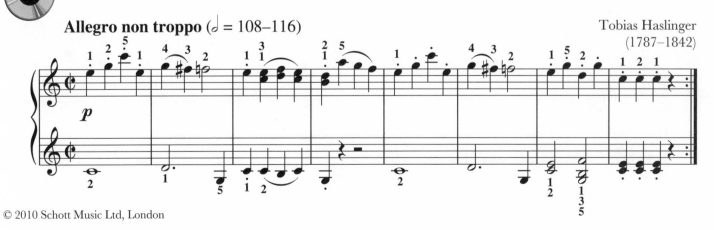

11. Deutscher Tanz

WoO 42 No. 1

Ludwig van Beethoven
(1770–1827)

Allegretto (♩ = 152–160)

mf

p

simile

12. Ecossaise
WoO 86

Ludwig van Beethoven
(1770–1827)

13. Allegro
KV3

Wolfgang Amadeus Mozart
(1756–1791)

14. Minuet

KV5

Wolfgang Amadeus Mozart
(1756–1791)

15. Deutscher Tanz

Hob. IX: 12 No. 1

Joseph Haydn
(1732–1809)

16. Minuet

KV2

Wolfgang Amadeus Mozart
(1756–1791)

17

17. Sonatina
Op. 41 No. 1

Johann Baptist Vanhal
(1739–1813)

Cadenza

Arietta

Andante cantabile (♩ = 130–136)

Allegretto (♩ = 152–156)

18. Bourrée in E Minor

Leopold Mozart
(1719–1787)

19. Allegretto in C Major

Johann Baptist Cramer
(1771–1858)

20. Allemande

Op. 4 No. 9

Carl Maria von Weber
(1786–1826)

23. Eccosaise

(♩ = 118–124)

Johann Wilhelm Hässler
(1747–1822)

24. Cantabile in A Minor

Daniel Steibelt
(1765–1823)

(♩ = 42–46)

25. Praeludium & Air Russe*

Praeludium

($\quad$ = 116–120)

Johann Baptist Cramer
(1771–1858)

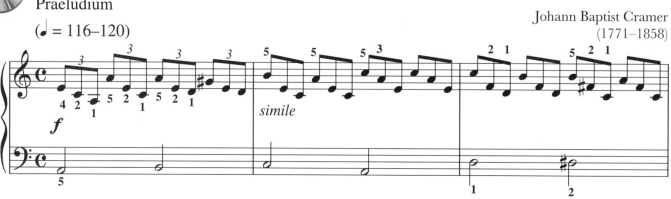

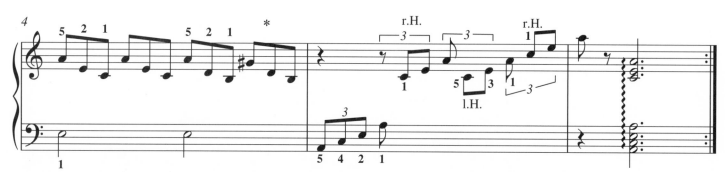

*Fingering is the composer's own / Le doigté sont du compositeur / Der Fingersatz stammt von Komponisten

Air Russe

26. Air Russe *

Johann Nepomuk Hummel
(1778–1837)

* Fingering is the composer's own / Le doigté sont du compositeur / Der Fingersatz stammt von Komponisten

27. Siciliano in G Minor

August Eberhard Müller
(1767–1817)

• aus / from / de : F. Emonts (ed.), Leichte Klavierstücke / Easy Piano Pieces / Pièces faciles pour piano, Schott ED 4747

© 2010 Schott Music Ltd, London

28. Ecossaise
WoO 23

Ludwig van Beethoven
(1770–1827)

Allegtetto (♩ = 118–124)

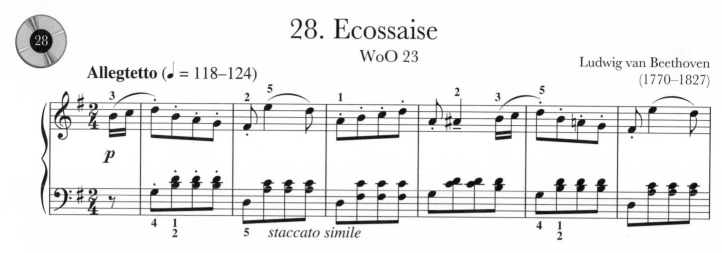

staccato simile

staccato simile

29. Ecossaise
D145 No. 4

Franz Schubert
(1797–1828)

30. Deutscher Tanz
D972 No. 3

Franz Schubert
(1797–1828)

Printed in Germany • S&Co. 8548

Teaching Notes

One of the interesting challenges of playing music of this period is how we negotiate the difference between the fortepiano of the late 18th century and the piano of today. These differences are quite considerable, but incorporating the knowledge of period instruments while playing modern pianos can only enhance how we respond to the music. For example, the piano in the classical period had lighter keys (and fewer of them), strings that ran parallel to each other as opposed to being cross-strung, leather not felt on its hammer, slighter proportions, no metal frame and a different action, too. All of this means that we can't recreate a sound as Haydn or Mozart may have heard it, but we can play the modern piano in a way that is respectful of these other musical textures. To achieve that, you might want to use sharply contrasted dynamic differences between forte and piano, and treat the right pedal as something that enhances the music at specific points, rather than being ever present. The basic sound quality should also be focused more on the treble of the instrument, rather than being bass orientated. Ornamentation too is important and the CD recording contains the occasional ornament at a cadential point. The use of ornaments is often a matter of personal choice and maybe the best way to think of ornaments is as a subtle enhancing of a melody line.

Ultimately, the concept of historically informed performance practice (being aware of and influenced by an understanding of how music of a different period may have been played) is an excellent basis for experimenting with music, for listening, evaluating and decision-making.

Ludwig van Beethoven

11. Deutscher Tanz WoO42 No. 1
(♩ = 152–160)

This *Allemande*, or *German Dance*, dates from the mid 1790s and was published in 1814 as one of six Allemandes for piano and violin. The piano solo version was first published in 1855, and it is possible that the transcription (which is essentially an omission of the violin part) was made by the editor, W. Plachy. The main challenge of the piece is the synchronizing of right hand crotchets and left hand quavers. Stay close to the keys, especially in the left hand, to ensure that both hands are coordinated. A very slight emphasis on the first beat of a bar will help project the feeling of a dance in 3/4 time.

12. Ecossaise WoO 86
(♩ = 152–160)

Beethoven's manuscript is dated 14th November 1825, making this one of the composer's later works. There is no original tempo indication, but the musical sense of one strong beat per bar establishes some tempo parameters. As so often with album leaf-type compositions such as this, the autograph contains some, but not all articulation details. The dotted lines are editorial, and are as such only optional. Some chord and single note coordination issues between both hands need to be prepared carefully, as the key signature of E-flat major requires the right hand to assume positions where the thumb sometimes covers white, and sometimes black, notes. Having to move one's hand around in such a way is good preparation for future repertoire in which this skill is needed.

28. Ecossaise WoO 23
(♩ = 118–124)

This work was published in 1810 in a publication calling itself The *Musical Penny Magazine (Musikalisches Pfennigmagazin)*: a publication of very short miniatures by a range of named and anonymous composers, seemingly available at a budget price. Beethoven's lively Scottish dance is in three sections, of which the first and third are identical. The octave jumps in the left hand (bars 9–12) should sound quite firm, yet still *staccato*. Bars 13 and 14 contain accents on off-beats that mirror the rhythmic pattern of the melody line in bars 2 and 4. To develop a secure left hand (and your stretch permitting), you can practise the left-hand notes of each of the opening bars as chords before playing the piece as written:

Johann Baptist Cramer

19. Allegretto in C Major
(♩. = 72–76)

Both this and the following piece by Cramer are taken from the 'School Edition', i.e. a condensed version of his piano method. Cramer suggests that he would like to introduce 'musical basics, including playing in the most frequently used keys, in 41 lessons'[1]. The fingering in this piece is the composer's. The character of the work is that of a short etude, a piece written to sound good and introduce its player to a specific skill. In the case of this *Allegretto*, it is the evenness of the semiquaver passage work that seems to be the most important element. Once learnt, the work can be used for a number of purposes: as part of a warming up routine or as the basis for experimenting with transposition.

25. Praeludium & Air Russe
(♩ = 116–120), (♩ = 96–104)

Coming from the same publication as the above Allegretto, *Praeludium & Air Russe* uses a concept that can also be found on Vanhal's *Sonatina* Op. 41 No. 1 in this book (track 17). It was customary in the late 18th and early 19th century for pianists to prepare their audience for what they were about to hear, usually by means of a brief introduction or improvisation in the key of the subsequent piece. The present *Praeludium* does exactly that. You can hear the underlying minor chord progression of the prelude if you play each group of triplets as a crotchet chord. The *Air Russe* is Cramer's version of a Russian song known at the time as *Schöne Minka* ('Beautiful Minka'). It was also used by Weber as the theme for his variations Op. 40 (1815), and by Beethoven in his folk song variations Op. 107 (1820). Cramer's version is a useful study in playing and pedalling 6ths.

Anton Diabelli

4. Piano piece Op. 125 No. 7
(♩. = 120–124)

Training the left hand to anticipate chord changes is an important part of learning this piece. You can achieve this by playing all left hand notes as a chord (one per bar) whilst playing the right hand as written. Once this is more readily achieved, separate the notes

1 Cramer, J. B., *Anweisung das Piano-Forte zu spielen*, (Offenbach: Johann André, No.3661, no date)

of the left hand as written. Articulation in the right hand is largely straight forward, except the reoccurring idea in bar three:

To achieve this sound, imagine the notation to be this, and it'll sound right:

5. *Piano piece Op. 125 No. 6*
(♩. = 112–116)

The left hand has sustained notes in the lower line and changing notes in the upper line in bars 1,2,13 and 14. To help develop this coordination skill, practise the following a few times before playing these bars as written:

Johann Wilhelm Hässler
23. Ecossaise in G Major
(♩ = 118–124)

This is an excellent piece for performance due to its catchy melody and crisp rhythm. To project the latter, place emphasis on the quavers (which are on the beats), rather than the first of the semiquaver patterns. It will also make each group of three slurred notes sound more even. To get the best sense of togetherness in the thirds in bars 9–12, practise them slowly as repeated semiquavers, rather than individual quavers; it somehow helps the fingers balance the thirds more effectively. Finally, in slow practice do exaggerate the difference between legato and staccato notes so that when the piece is up to speed, your audience can still tell the difference between joint and detached notes.

Tobias Haslinger
10. Sonatina in C Major
(♩ = 108–116)

Similarly to Hässler's Eccosaise, this sonatina requires contrast between legato and staccato notes. The musical articulation should be incorporated from the very first learning stages, since it is an integral part of the piece. To make the quavers in bar 11 very smooth, especially at the point of crossing over with the third finger, move your elbow outwards ever so slightly to support the crossing of the third finger.

Joseph Haydn
8. Deutscher Tanz Hob. IX:8
(♩ = 152–156)

This *Allemande* does not need to be too fast, especially as the difference between slurred and detached notes needs to be very clear. To achieve this, take a look at the fingering in bars 2 to 3. It might be unconventional to re-use the third finger on successive quavers across the bar line, but it does help to underline the slurring as notated by Haydn. If you do decide to use this fingering, make the C quite light and short, and move the third finger to the B with minimal loss of key contact. Are there easier ways to play this? Try the fingering in brackets. Ultimately it's the sound of the melody line that determines how you might want to play this.

15. Deutscher Tanz Hob. IX:12
(♩. = 66–72)

If your fingers almost cover all the quavers in a bar at the point of playing the first of each group (i.e. bar), you'll have no problems getting this dance up to speed quite soon.

22. Kontretanz Hob. XXXIc:17b
(♩ = 60–66)

Written in London, this dance is the piano version of a piece originally written for larger ensemble. The suggested fingering in bar 3 implies a slurring in two quavers. If you want to change this sound, you might have to change the fingering too.

Johann Nepomuk Hummel
9. Ecossaise Op. 52 No. 5
(♩ = 160–164)

Taken from the collection of 6 easy pieces Op. 52, this is by far the shortest work of the set. Ever since its publication the Ecossaise has been included in many piano teaching books. Make a strong contrast between the piano sound of the first line and the fortissimo beginning of the second. It is meant to be very firm, so enjoy making a big sound! The held-on bass line of the second half might need some extra attention. In this texture you might find it useful to hold the lower voice, and to practice the quavers as staccato notes at the same time. It makes the task more difficult, but the end result much more convincing, once you return to playing both lines legato.

26. Un poco adagio (Air Russe)
(♩ = 60–66)

It's a very short piece, but also a rather beautiful melody. The emphasis is on legato playing, and on hearing each of the three voices (or parts) progress from one note to the next.

August Eberhard Müller
27. Siciliano in G Minor
(♩. = 52–56)

This piece is taken from Müller's collection of 'Instructive Practice Pieces for the Pianoforte' (*Instruktive übungsstücke für das Pianoforte*), one of the leading piano methods of its time. The works seems to exist in alternative versions in a and g minor. Apart from the odd dynamic marking, the score leaves much to the imagination of the player.

Leopold Mozart

1. Minuet in D Minor
(♩ = 144–152)

The score contains no dynamic or articulation markings, thus giving the performer the opportunity to shape this work according to their musical taste. For the purpose of the recording, I have chosen to play the quavers as legato patterns, but this is an option, not a requirement. You could slur the quavers in groups of two, particularly if you prefer playing this piece at a slightly slower tempo. Whatever the outcome of these decisions, the really interesting aspect of learning this piece is the opportunity for experimentation and subsequent decision making.

2. Minuet in F Major
(♩ = 156–162)

Again, the score gives plenty of opportunities for experimentation and decision making in terms of articulation and the use of dynamics. To emphasise the first beat in a bar, I have joined the first and second beats in bars 1, 3 and 5.

7. Minuet in C Major
(♩ = 132–136)

Just as the previous two pieces, this work comes from Leopold Mozart's *Note Book* of 1759, and was written for his daughter Nannerl. To make an effective difference between the use of semiquavers and triplets in this piece, sharpen the rhythm of the dotted quaver to semiquaver ever so slightly by delaying the latter.

18. Bourée in E Minor
(♩ = 70–76)

This *Bourée* can be approached in several different ways. You could play all crotchets slightly detached and all groups of quavers slurred in groups of two. On the other hand, you might prefer to slur some groups of crotchets, too. Providing this is done with the basic pulse of the piece in mind, it is also a good solution.

Wolfgang Amadeus Mozart

3. Minuet KV 6/IIIa (♩ = 136–140)
6. Minuet KV 1e (♩ = 120–128)
13. Allegro KV3 (♩ = 60–66)
14. Minuet KV5 (♩ = 120–126)
16. Minuet KV2 (♩. = 50–56)

These pieces are amongst Mozart's earliest compositions, and were almost certainly written under the supervision of his father Leopold. Most of the scores have little in terms of performance directions, so it is up to the performer to chose a dynamic framework, as well as appropriate forms of articulation. In general terms, it is probably reasonable to detach all longer notes from each other, as long as they are not specifically slurred. Quavers can be slurred in groups of two or three, depending on the context. Considering the dynamic range of early fortepianos, terraced dynamics of *forte* and *piano* are stylistically in keeping, as might be the occasional crescendo or decrescendo over a few notes. The use of the pedal is also possible, though again it should be done sparingly and discreetly.

Franz Schubert

29. Ecossaise Op. 18 No. 4 (D145)
(♩ = 80–84)

This *Ecossaise* is as boisterous as it is short. A firm sound, direct touch and good supporting base chords will contribute to making this piece sound impressive.

30. Deutscher Tanz D. 972 No. 3
(♩ = 60–66)

This *German dance* is probably a little more intricate than it sounds, particularly in its quaver sequences in the right hand. You can support the first beat in each bar with the use of the pedal, which underlines the dance-like quality of the work in a subtle manner. The last beat of bar 12 should serve as an upbeat into bar 13.

Daniel Steibelt

24. Cantabile in A Minor
(♩ = 42–46)

Steibelt's work is a fine example of music written on the verge of the classical to the romantic period. Its distinct melodic line has a vocal quality to it that needs prominence, even when played by the left hand in bars 17–20.

Johann Baptist Vanhal

17. Sonatina Op. 41 No. 1
Arietta (♩ = 130–136), *Allegretto* (♩ = 152–156)

Vanhal's work is the first of a series of *12 Sonatinas faciles et progressives* Op. 41. Its musical qualities apart, the piece is of interest for two quite specific reasons. Firstly, it opens with a brief cadential prelude that establishes the key of C major, a reflection of contemporaneous performance practice of the period. Secondly, it offers a complete sonatina on one page, enabling students at this stage of their development to play a work in two movements. Compared to the musical detail of the two movements, the Cadenza section merely offers the notes, which can be understood as an invitation to personalize the music, or even improvise around the given text, as players of the time might have done.

Carl Maria von Weber

20. Allemande Op. 4 No. 9 (♩ = 132–138)
21. Allemande Op. 4 No. 2 (♩ = 140–144)

Weber's Allemandes are taken from a collection of *12 Allemandes* Op. 4. In No. 9, you might have to omit the G in the left hand for two beats in order to allow the melody note of the right hand to be heard. In bars 7 and 15 of No. 2, the thumb should wait under the other fingers as you start the quaver pattern and thus be ready to play the third quaver in the bar.

Nils Franke

Biographical Notes

Ludwig van Beethoven (1770–1827)

Beethoven's influence on the direction of music in his time, as well as on the musical developments of subsequent composers, was considerable and multi-layered. His own stylistic development as a composer has resulted in the categorizing of his output into three distinct periods: up to about 1802 (early), from 1802–1812 (middle), and from 1812 onwards (late). In terms of Beethoven's piano writing, these periods reflect the classical heritage of his initial phase, the development of his virtuoso keyboard style, and the subsequent structural, as well as technical individuality of his later works.

As a composer, Beethoven excelled in almost all forms of instrumental music, from the string quartet, the piano sonata, to the concerto and the symphony. The spontaneity, strength and emotional impact of his music were nevertheless the result of a meticulously crafted process of composition that is documented in detail in his sketchbooks and autographs. Beethoven was a successful performer as a pianist, though contemporary accounts of his playing differ in their assessment, depending on the focus of the writers. While some praised Beethoven's power and sound projection, others thought his playing to be messy and lacking control. What most sources agree upon though, is the impact Beethoven's playing made upon his listeners.

A piano work that unites both perspectives of his playing is the *Fantasy* for piano Op. 77; a work that is largely understood to be the written down version of an improvisation. It contains many Beethovenian features in harmony, melody and texture, and can as such offer a unique insight into the workings of this great musician.

Beethoven's compositional achievements were so considerable that subsequent generations of composers from Schubert to Schumann, Liszt and Brahms hesitated for some time before writing in a genre that Beethoven had previously made his own.

Johann Baptist Cramer (1771–1858)

Born in Germany, Cramer was taken to England at the age of three by his family. In 1783 he studied with Muzio Clementi for a year, whose style of piano playing became a major influence on Cramer in the development of his own pianism. Indeed, Cramer became known amongst colleagues and audiences for the quality of his legato touch. As Clementi did before him, Cramer managed to combine a career as a performer, teacher and musical businessman, becoming involved in music publishing from 1805 onwards. These seemingly diverse roles were not uncommon amongst musicians in the second half of the 18th century, especially as the writing and publishing of educational music in particular was a lucrative market. Cramer's *84 Studies* for piano (published in two sets of 42 in 1804 and 1810), aimed at just such an audience, were as commercially successful as they were pianistically influential. Beethoven recommended them for the development of piano technique (he annotated selected Cramer Etudes, highlighting their individual musical purposes), Schumann used them, Henselt composed a second piano part to them, and Liszt's student Carl Tausig (one of the 19th century's most celebrated pianists) edited a selection of Cramer Etudes, thus underlining their relevance about half a century after they first appeared in print.

Cramer's life pre 1800 seems to have consisted of teaching piano and going on concert tours across parts of Europe. Post 1800, he remained mostly England-based, concentrating on his music publishing business and composition. Cramer retired in 1835 as a highly respected member of London's musical life.

Anton Diabelli (1781–1858)

Nowadays, Diabelli's name is principally remembered for two things: sonatinas (and there are quite a few of them) and providing a theme to Beethoven, on which the latter based his most extensive piano cycle, the *Diabelli Variations* Op.120. These works highlight two successful parts of Diabelli's life; that of a composing instrumental teacher who wrote skilfully for his student population and the shrewd music publisher who invited 50 of Austria's most respected composers to provide him with a variation, based on his own theme. Beethoven, rather famously, did not provide what was asked for, nor when it was requested, but eventually produced an extraordinary fifty-five minute set of variations.

Diabelli's publishing house built its success on achieving a balance between issuing many commercial works, as well as championing music by Beethoven and Schubert, whose earliest printed works were published by Diabelli.

Johann Wilhelm Hässler (1747–1822)

Born in Erfurt in 1747, Hässler became a student of his uncle, the Erfurt organist Johann Christian Kittel. By the age of 16, Hässler held his first appointment as an organist in Erfurt but soon began to travel across Germany as a concertizing musician. In 1780 he founded his own music publishing business and by 1790 had travelled as far afield as England and Russia, where he became the court conductor in St. Petersburg in 1792. In a letter from 1788, the poet and writer Friedrich von Schiller recalls Hässler's playing: 'He plays like a master and composes very well. As a person, he is an original and a rather fiery being.'[1] From 1794 onwards, Hässler lived in Moscow where he worked as a highly respected and sought-after piano teacher. His contribution to the development of Russian pianism in the first half of the 19th century is yet to be defined but most of his published works for piano suggest a clear focus on developing the skills of less experienced players.

Hässler's own keyboard style developed from the piano writing of C. P. E. Bach but shares the accessibility of Haydn's earlier piano sonatas. Many of Hässler's smaller teaching pieces and easier piano sonatas benefit from their immediate musical appeal, and his piano method contains many works that can still be used today.

Tobias Haslinger (1787–1842)

His early training as a chorister in Linz enabled Haslinger to learn a number of different instruments. After moving to Vienna in 1810 he began to self-publish some of his own compositions before joining the music publisher S.A. Stainer as an employee. Increasingly, his compositional activities (totalling around 100 works from shorter piano pieces to two masses) appear to have given way to his business interests. Haslinger's musical judgement and his personal contact to composers such as Beethoven, and later Johann Strauss and Liszt, enabled his publishing house to flourish. By 1826 he owned the company that now took his name. An advertisement at the time lists some 5000 musical items as being in his company catalogue. Haslinger's business success seems to have coincided with the growing popularity of

---

1 Kahl, W., *Selbstbiographien Deutscher Musiker* (Koeln und Krefeld, Staufen Verlag, 1948), p.47

the Viennese waltz, and his publishing of two of its most illustrious exponents, Johann Strauss and Lanner.

Joseph Haydn (1732–1809)

The evaluation of Haydn's position as a composer has undergone a number of changes over time. A popular perception of Haydn's life is the focus on the relative comfort and stability of his almost 30 year employment by the Esterhazy family in Eisenstadt near Vienna. Despite this comparatively settled existence (at least compared to that of many of his contemporaries, not least Mozart), Haydn's music was published widely post 1780, gaining its composer a growing national and international reputation. Visits to London from 1791 onwards confirmed his musical and economic successes. However, his early years were very different. After initial training as a chorister and violinist, Haydn, who was not a virtuoso performer, survived by teaching and playing in ad hoc ensembles that provided music for functions. Compositionally, Haydn progressed slowly from being essentially self-taught to gaining the necessary skills. From the mid 1760s onwards Haydn developed a more distinctive musical style.

Haydn's output for piano covers over 60 sonatas, individual pieces, and variations. Though not a virtuoso keyboard performer, Haydn knew exactly how to write effectively for the fortepiano. All of his works lie very well under the fingers (irrespective of their varying degrees of complexity), but it is the element of surprise, both harmonically and in terms of pianistic textures, that gives many of the pieces their particular charm. Haydn's piano writing is never formulaic and therefore ever so slightly unpredictable.

Johann Nepomuk Hummel (1778–1837)

Hummel was arguably a pivotal figure in his time, both pianistically and compositionally. A pupil of Mozart, Hummel's music always retained its classical roots in terms of its structure and musical detail. Yet as a pianist, and maybe most importantly as an influential piano teacher, Hummel trained many exponents of the first generation of 19th century pianism: Henselt, Hiller, Mendelssohn and Thalberg all benefitted from Hummel's tuition. Other pianists of the time were also influenced by Hummel. Schumann considered studying with him (he didn't in the end) but Hummel's decorative right hand figurations clearly occupied Schumann, as the *Abegg Variations* Op. 1 and other early works document. Liszt, too, came into contact with Hummel's music by playing the latter's *Piano Concerti* Opp. 85 and 89 early on in his career as a travelling virtuoso. Even Chopin must have been familiar with Hummel's works, as some of his earlier pieces display some stylistic, occasionally even melodic, similarities.

One of Hummel's outstanding achievements is his piano method of 1828, a 450+ page document that claims to train the student 'from the first lesson to the most complete training'[1]. Published by Tobias Haslinger (see piece No. 10 in this anthology) in Vienna, it is possibly the 19th century's first comprehensive piano method book that established the technical concepts upon which the virtuoso pianism of that century were based. Hummel's thorough training methodology apart, what makes this method quite remarkable is its author's awareness of and perspective on aspects of pedagogy: student-teacher interaction, motivation, and lesson delivery are amongst the topics that Hummel explores.

August Eberhard Müller (1767–1817)

Müller seems to have been a teacher-performer-composer whose work was very highly regarded in his time. A pianist, organist and flautist by training, Müller became assistant to (1800) and successor of (1804) J.A. Hiller as Kantor of the Thomaskirche in Leipzig, a position previously held by, amongst others, J.S. Bach. In 1810 he was appointed as the court conductor (Kapellmeister) in Weimar. As a composer of educational material, Müller wrote for flute as well as piano, the latter with considerable success. Though his pianoforte method of 1804 was an updated and extended version of the *Pianoforteschule* by Loehlein, its success is illustrated by the fact that in 1825 Carl Czerny oversaw the new edition of Müller's method; and the Parisian piano virtuoso Friedrich Kalkbrenner based his own piano tutor book on Müller's. Unsurprisingly, individual pieces of his were available throughout much of the 19th century. As a performer, Müller directed works by many of his contemporaries (such as Haydn's *The Creation* in 1801) and as a scholar, he wrote about performance practice of Mozart's piano concerti (1797).

Leopold Mozart (1719–1787)

Though mostly remembered today for being the father of W.A. Mozart, Leopold Mozart was a distinguished musician, composer and educator in his own right. After initially studying philosophy, Mozart's musical activities became increasingly important to him. Over a period of twenty years he progressed from a first violinist (sitting number four) to deputy Kapellmeister in the court orchestra of Archbishop Leopold Freiherr von Firmian in Salzburg. He also taught violin and keyboard, leading to the publication of his highly regarded *Violin Method* in 1756. Mozart's ability to write effective music for learners is particularly well documented in the note books for his two children, Nannerl and Wolfgang Amadeus. His compositional output included numerous symphonies, serenades, concerti and keyboard pieces, though many works are now considered lost. Of the pieces that have survived, his dances and smaller works for keyboard are arguably the most frequently performed.

Wolfgang Amadeus Mozart (1756–1791)

Mozart was born into a highly musical environment. His father Leopold worked as an orchestral violinist and educator in Salzburg, and his older sister Nannerl had already shown her ability as a keyboard player. Mozart made rapid progress in his musical studies, so much so that his father decided to take him on a concert tour through Germany to London and Paris. These travels lasted for three and a half years before Mozart settled into life in Salzburg in 1766. Annual travels to Italy followed from 1769–72, enabling Mozart to come into contact with many other musicians, as indeed he did throughout his life. By the early 1780s Mozart seemed to have settled into life as a freelance musician in all its diversity. Some of his most successful piano concerti date from this period, as do many string quartets, some of which he played alongside their dedicatee, Joseph Haydn. By the end of the decade (and the beginning of the next) Mozart enjoyed considerable success as an opera composer with works such as *Cosi fan tutte* and *Die Zauberflöte*.

The diversity of Mozart's keyboard writing naturally reflects the different periods in the composer's life. Some of the earliest works date from when he was only five, a time when he wrote mostly shorter dances. His mature works include sonatas, variations and individual pieces, many of them written for his own use.

---

1 Hummel, J. N., *Anweisung zum Piano-forte spielen* (Wien: Haslinger, 1828)

Franz Schubert (1797–1828)

Schubert's initial musical training was provided by his father and brothers who taught him to play the piano, violin and viola. Aged 11 he was awarded a choral scholarship that enabled him to study with Salieri. By the age of 16, Schubert decided to train as a teacher and a year later started work at his father's school. Aged 17, Schubert had written some of his early masterpieces, *Erlkönig* and *Gretchen am Spinnrade* for voice and piano. In 1816 Schubert relinquished his teaching post, choosing instead to live in the Viennese city centre and concentrating on composition. A period of financial uncertainty followed, but late in 1819 Schubert wrote his first larger scale chamber music masterpiece, the Trout Quintet. In spring 1821 the success of the *Erlkönig* led to publications of his songs by Diabelli, and from it Schubert experienced a brief period of financial stability. From 1820–23 he was preoccupied by writing operatic music, a less than successful venture, only to turn to writing chamber and symphonic works for the last three years of his life.

Schubert's piano writing is, with few exceptions, not preoccupied with some of the outwardly technical components that some of his contemporaries employed. Instead, much of the music's demands arise from its preference of musical purpose over any form of pianistic display.

Daniel Steibelt (1765–1823)

Much of Steibelt's life reflects the circumstances that several performer-composers of the time experienced. Born in one country, and living and working in several others, Steibelt, like Hässler and Field, eventually moved to Russia. Steibelt's personality and business dealings may in themselves have necessitated a comparatively regular change of environment. Contemporaries report a vain and extravagant character, as well as some personally crooked tendencies. Unpaid debts and breaches of contracts gave Steibelt a colourful reputation, as did his tendency to sell marginally altered works (mostly of his own) as new compositions. That Steibelt could play the piano well is rarely disputed, yet as a composer most of his works tend to reflect a contemporaneous demand for fashionable music. Where Steibelt is arguably at his best is in the genre of the short character piece for piano, whether a study or a prelude. As much of the musical content is driven by pianistic invention and presented in a relatively condensed format, Steibelt's miniatures can be unusually effective. Works of particular interest to piano students and teachers include his piano tutor book *Methode* (1805) and *50 Etudes* Op. 78.

Johann Baptist Vanhal (1739–1813)

The Bohemian composer Vanhal trained as a singer and violinist (later also as a keyboard player) before moving to Vienna at the age of 21. There he worked as private instrumental tutor, teaching amongst others, the young Ignace Pleyel. In 1769 he embarked on a two-year tour of Italy before returning to Vienna. As a composer, Vanhal appears to have worked in different genres at specific times. By 1780, he had turned away from writing symphonies and a few years later stopped writing string quartets, concentrating instead on keyboard music and sacred works. The extent to which his works were published in his lifetime establishes Vanhal as an important musical figure, though quite a few of his works have remained in manuscript. As such, a comprehensive perspective of his achievements may still be pending.

Carl Maria von Weber (1786–1826)

Weber's early life is typical of that of many musicians of his time. Receiving his initial musical instruction from his father and several local musicians, Weber's travels around Germany and Austria put him in touch with Michael Haydn (Joseph's brother and a highly respected composer in his own right) and the composer and theorist Georg Joseph Vogler who provided much of the systematic tuition Weber needed. Until 1810, Weber moved from place to place, holding down a succession of musical and, in some cases, administrative positions. A court case against Weber and his father, being placed under civil arrest and, ultimately, banned from the area of Württemberg had a profound effect on Weber. Determined to change his life, he embarked on two years of composing, concertizing and living within his means. Appointments as court and/or theatre conductor soon followed; Prague from 1813–16 and Dresden from 1817–1821; periods during which he also continued to travel as a performing musician. Arguably the most significant change in Weber's life occurred due to the extraordinary popularity of his opera *Der Freischütz* (1820), a work that secured him success throughout Germany, as well as internationally.

Weber's piano writing is distinctive, yet also difficult to summarise. It is clearly melodically driven, as is much of Weber's homophonic writing, with a particular emphasis on dance forms and dotted rhythmic patterns that underpin his compositional style. As a pianist, Weber is drawn to elaborate and often virtuosic right hand writing; fast moving chord progressions, hand crossing and leaps that go far beyond a hand position. In that sense, Weber's piano writing is based on the fluid scale and arpeggio technique favoured by Hummel, but occupies a halfway position between the latter and the pianism demanded by Chopin and Liszt from the 1830s onwards.

Notes pédagogiques

L'un des enjeux intéressants dans l'interprétation de la musique de cette période réside dans la négociation des différences entre le pianoforte de la fin du 18e siècle et le piano actuel. Ces différences sont assez considérables, mais l'intégration de notre connaissance des instruments d'époque ne peut qu'enrichir la réponse que nous apportons à cette musique lorsque nous la jouons sur un piano moderne. Par exemple, les touches du piano de la période classique étaient plus légères (et moins nombreuses), ses cordes disposées parallèlement et non croisées, ses marteaux recouverts de cuir et non de feutre ; il était de proportions plus réduites, n'avait pas de cadre métallique et possédait également un autre mécanisme. Cela signifie que nous ne pouvons recréer les sonorités telles que Mozart ou Haydn les entendaient, mais nous pouvons jouer du piano moderne en respectant ces textures musicales différentes. Afin d'y parvenir, il vous faudra user de contrastes dynamiques très différenciés entre *piano* et *forte* et traiter la pédale de droite comme un moyen d'enrichir ponctuellement la musique plutôt que de l'utiliser en permanence.

Fondamentalement, la qualité sonore devra être axée davantage sur les aigus de l'instrument que sur les graves. L'ornementation est également importante et l'enregistrement figurant sur le CD contient des ornementations occasionnelles dans les passages cadentiels. L'utilisation des ornements est souvent une question de choix personnel dans l'enrichissement subtil d'une ligne mélodique. Enfin, le concept d'une pratique musicale historiquement éclairée (conscience et influence de la compréhension des pratiques musicales d'une époque différente) constitue une base excellente à l'expérimentation musicale, pour l'écoute, l'évaluation et les choix musicaux.

Ludwig van Beethoven
11. Deutscher Tanz WoO42 no 1
(♩ = 152–160)

Cette *Allemande*, ou *Danse allemande*, date du milieu des années 1790 et fut publiée en 1814 parmi un ensemble de six allemandes pour piano et violon. La version pour piano seul ne fut publiée qu'en 1855 et il est possible que la transcription (qui réside essentiellement dans l'omission de la partie de violon) ait été réalisée par l'éditeur, W. Plachy. L'enjeu principal de cette pièce est de synchroniser les noires de la main droite et les croches de la main gauche. Restez proches des touches, en particulier à la main gauche, afin d'assurer la coordination des deux mains. Une très légère emphase sur le premier temps de la mesure accentuera la sensation d'une danse à 3/4.

12. Écossaise WoO 86
(♩ = 152–160)

Le manuscrit de Beethoven est daté du 14 novembre 1825, faisant de cette composition l'une de ses œuvres les plus tardives. Il n'y a pas d'indication de tempo originale, mais la sensation musicale d'un temps fort par mesure permet d'établir quelques paramètres de tempo. Comme cela est fréquent dans le cas de courtes pages d'albums comme celle-ci, le manuscrit autographe contient quelques détails d'articulation, mais pas tous. Les liaisons tiretées ont été ajoutées par l'éditeur et, en tant que telles, ne sont donc qu'optionnelles. La coordination des deux mains nécessite une préparation soigneuse pour certains accords, voire certaines notes isolées, dans la mesure où, du fait de la tonalité de mi bémol

majeur, la main droite occupe des positions où le pouce enfonce alternativement des touches blanches et des touches noires. Devoir déplacer ainsi sa main constitue une bonne préparation au répertoire futur, dans lequel cette faculté est nécessaire.

28. Écossaise WoO 23
(♩ = 118–124)

Cette œuvre parut en 1810 dans une publication nommée le *Musikalisches Pfennigmagazin* (*Magazine musical à quatre sous*) qui proposait pour un prix apparemment dérisoire de très courtes miniatures dues à toute une série de compositeurs reconnus ou anonymes. Cette danse écossaise animée de Beethoven s'articule en trois parties dont la première et la troisième sont identiques. Les sauts d'octaves de la main gauche (mesures 9–12) doivent sonner avec fermeté, mais toujours *staccato*. Les mesures 13 et 14 présentent des accents sur des temps faibles, reprenant le motif rythmique de la ligne mélodique aux mesures 2 et 4. Afin de développer l'assurance de la main gauche (et vos capacités d'extension), vous pouvez vous entraîner à jouer les notes de la main gauche des mesures d'ouverture sous forme d'accords avant de jouer la pièce comme elle est écrite :

Johann Baptist Cramer
19. Allegretto en ut majeur
(♩. = 72–76)

Cette pièce de Cramer ainsi que la suivante sont tirées de la « School edition » (édition scolaire), c'est à dire d'une version condensée de sa méthode de piano. Cramer indique qu'il souhaite y présenter « les bases de la musique, y compris le jeu dans les tonalités les plus usitées, en 41 leçons »[1]. Les doigtés de cette pièce sont ceux du compositeur. Le caractère de l'œuvre est celui d'une courte étude, une pièce écrite pour sonner bien et initier son interprète à une compétence particulière. Dans le cas de cet *Allegretto*, l'élément le plus important semble résider dans la régularité du passage en double croches. Une fois apprise, cette œuvre peut être utilisée à différents effets : comme élément d'échauffement ou comme base pour s'exercer à la transposition.

25. Prélude & air russe
(♩ = 116–120), (♩ = 96–104)

Issus de la même publication que l'Allegretto ci-dessus, les *Prélude & Air Russe* s'appuient sur un concept que l'on trouve également dans la *Sonatine* op. 41 no 1 de Vanhal figurant dans ce recueil (piste 17). À la fin du 18e siècle et au début du 19e, il était d'usage pour les pianistes de préparer leur auditoire à ce qu'il était sur le point d'entendre, habituellement par le biais d'une brève introduction ou d'une improvisation dans la tonalité de la pièce considérée. C'est exactement le rôle du *Prélude* dont il est question ici. Vous pourrez entendre la progression d'accords en mineur sous-tendant le prélude en jouant chaque triolet sous forme d'accord, sur la durée d'une noire. *L'Air russe* repose sur la version de Cramer d'une chanson russe connue alors sous le titre de *Schöne Minka* (*La belle Minka*). Celle-ci a étalement été utilisée par Weber comme thème

---

1 Cramer, J. B., *Anweisung das Piano-Forte zu spielen* (Offenbach : Johann André, no 3661, non daté)

de ses variations op. 40 (1815) et par Beethoven dans ses variations sur une chanson populaire op. 107 (1820). La version de Cramer est une étude utile pour travailler et « pédaliser » les sixtes.

Anton Diabelli

4. Pièce pour piano op. 125 no 7
(♩. = 120–124)
Entraîner la main gauche à anticiper les changements d'accords constitue une part importante de l'apprentissage de cette pièce. Vous pouvez y parvenir en jouant toutes les notes de la main gauche sous forme d'accord (un par mesure) tout en exécutant la main droite telle qu'elle est écrite. Lorsque vous y parvenez sans difficulté, séparez les notes de la main gauche comme cela est écrit. L'articulation de la main droite ne présente pas de difficulté, hormis la récurrence de l'idée de la mesure 3 :

Afin de réaliser cette sonorité, imaginez que la notation se présente comme suit, et cela sonnera comme il faut :

5. Pièce pour piano op. 125 no 6
(♩. = 112–116)
Aux mesures 1, 2, 13 et 14, la main gauche présente des notes tenues à la ligne inférieure et des notes changeantes à la ligne supérieure. Afin de favoriser le développement de ces compétences de coordination, faites l'exercice suivant plusieurs fois avant d'exécuter ces mesures telles qu'elles sont écrites :

Johann Wilhelm Hässler

23. Écossaise en sol majeur
(♩ = 118–124)
Sa mélodie entraînante et ses rythmes animés font de cette écossaise une excellente pièce à jouer en public. Afin de bien réaliser les rythmes, placez l'accent sur les croches (sur les temps) plutôt que sur le premier motif en doubles-croches. Cela permettra également de faire sonner chaque groupe de trois notes liées de manière plus égale. Afin d'obtenir une meilleure sensation d'ensemble dans les tierces des mesures 9 à 12, entraînez-vous à les jouer lentement sous forme de doubles-croches répétées plutôt que comme des croches individuelles. Cela permet en quelque sorte aux doigts de mieux équilibrer les tierces. Enfin, lorsque vous jouez lentement, exagérez la différence entre *legato* et *staccato* afin que, lorsque vous jouerez la pièce à la bonne vitesse, votre auditoire soit toujours capable de

distinguer les notes liées des notes détachées.

Tobias Haslinger

10. Sonatine en ut majeur
(♩ = 108–116)
À l'instar de l'écossaise de Hässler, cette sonatine nécessite de bien contraster *staccato* et *legato*. L'articulation musicale sera intégrée dès les premiers stades de l'apprentissage, dans la mesure où elle fait partie intégrante de la pièce. Afin de réaliser les croches de la mesure 11 avec la douceur requise, en particulier à l'endroit de croisement du troisième doigt, écartez doucement votre coude vers l'extérieur pour soutenir ce croisement.

Joseph Haydn

8. Danse allemande Hob. IX:8
(♩ = 152–156)
Cette allemande n'a pas besoin d'être trop rapide, notamment parce que la différence entre les notes liées et les notes détachées doit rester clairement perceptible. Afin d'y parvenir, observez le doigté des mesures 2 et 3. Il n'est peut-être pas très conventionnel de réutiliser le troisième doigt sur des croches successives au passage de la barre de mesure, mais ce procédé permet de souligner les liaisons telles qu'elles sont notées par Haydn. Si vous décidez d'utiliser ce doigté, le *do* sera léger et bref, et le troisième doigt se déplacera vers le *si bémol* en restant le plus proche possible de la touche. Existe-t-il des moyens plus simples d'exécuter ce passage ? Essayez le doigté entre parenthèses. En dernier recours, c'est la sonorité de la ligne mélodique qui déterminera la façon dont vous jouerez ce passage.

15. Danse allemande Hob. IX:12
(♩. = 66–72)
Si vos doigts couvrent quasiment toutes les croches d'une mesure au moment de jouer la première de chaque groupe (c'est-à-dire de chaque mes.), vous n'éprouverez aucune difficulté à jouer rapidement cette danse à la vitesse requise.

22. Contredanse Hob. XXXIc:17b
(♩ = 60–66)
Écrite à Londres, cette danse est la version pour piano d'une pièce composée à l'origine pour un ensemble plus important. Le doigté proposé à la mesure 3 implique une liaison des croches deux par deux. Si vous souhaitez modifier cette sonorité, il vous faudra sans doute également changer de doigté.

Johann Nepomuk Hummel

9. Écossaise op. 52 no 5
(♩ = 160–164)
Tirée des 6 pièces faciles op. 52, c'est de loin la pièce la plus courte de ce volume. Cette écossaise a été intégrée dès sa publication à de nombreux ouvrages pédagogiques pour le *piano*. Faites bien contraster le piano de la première ligne et le *fortissimo* commençant à la seconde ligne. Celui-ci est censé être très marqué, alors n'hésitez pas à faire du bruit ! Les tenues de la ligne de basse requerront peut-être une attention particulière. Dans ce contexte, vous trouverez sans doute utile de tenir les notes de la voix inférieure et de jouer en même temps les croches *staccato*. Cela rend la tâche plus difficile, mais le résultat final sera beaucoup plus convaincant lorsque vous reprendrez les deux lignes *legato*.

26. Un poco adagio (Air russe)
(♩ = 60–66)
La pièce est très courte, mais la mélodie plutôt belle. Il faudra veiller à jouer *legato* et à entendre la progression des trois voix (ou parties) d'une note à l'autre.

August Eberhard Müller
27. Siciliano in sol mineur
(♩. = 52–56)
Cette pièce est tirée du recueil de Müller intitulé « Exercices instructifs pour le pianoforte » (*Instruktive Übungsstücke für das Pianoforte*), l'une des méthodes majeures de cette époque. Les œuvres existent dans deux versions différentes, en la et sol mineur. Hormis quelques indications dynamiques, la partition laisse beaucoup de place à l'imagination de l'interprète.

Leopold Mozart
1. Menuet en ré mineur
(♩ = 144–152)
La partition ne contient ni indications de dynamique ni d'articulation, laissant ainsi à l'interprète la possibilité de modeler cette œuvre selon ses goûts musicaux personnels. Pour les besoins de l'enregistrement, j'ai choisi de jouer les croches en motifs *legato*, mais il s'agit d'une option, non d'une exigence. Vous pouvez lier les croches par deux, en particulier si vous préférez jouer cette pièce à un tempo légèrement plus lent. Quelle que soit votre choix, l'aspect réellement intéressant dans l'apprentissage de cette pièce réside dans l'occasion qu'elle offre au pianiste d'expérimenter différentes options musicales et ainsi, de faire ses propres choix.

2. Menuet en fa majeur
(♩ = 156–162)
Là encore, la partition laisse une grande place à l'expérimentation et à la prise de décisions en termes d'articulation et d'utilisation des nuances. Afin de mettre l'accent sur le premier temps de la mesure, j'ai lié le premier et le second temps des mesures 1, 3 et 5.

7. Menuet en ut majeur
(♩ = 132–136)
Tout comme les deux pièces précédentes, cette œuvre est issue du carnet de notes de Léopold Mozart de 1759 et a été écrite pour sa fille Nannerl. Pour bien différencier l'utilisation des double-croches et des triolets dans cette pièce, il faudra très légèrement accentuer le rythme des motifs de croches pointées/doubles-croches en retardant ces dernières.

18. Bourrée in mi mineur
(♩ = 70–76)
Cette *bourrée* peut être abordée de différentes façons. Vous pouvez jouer toutes les noires légèrement détachées et toutes de croches liées par deux. Ou alors, vous préférerez peut-être lier également certains groupes de noires. À condition de le faire en gardant la pulsation fondamentale de la pièce à l'esprit, c'est également une bonne solution.

Wolfgang Amadeus Mozart
3. Minuet KV 6/IIIa (♩ = 136–140)
6. Minuet KV 1e (♩ = 120–128)
13. Allegro KV3 (♩ = 60–66)
14. Minuet KV5 (♩ = 120–126)
16. Minuet KV2 (♩. = 50–56)

Ces pièces comptent parmi les premières compositions de Mozart et ont presque certainement été écrites sous la direction de son père Léopold. La plupart des partitions ne comportent que peu d'indications de jeu si bien qu'il revient à l'interprète de choisir la structure dynamique ainsi que les formes d'articulation appropriées. De manière générale, et dans la mesure où il n'est pas spécifié qu'elles sont liées, il est probablement raisonnable de détacher toutes les notes longues les unes des autres. Les croches peuvent être liées par groupes de deux ou trois, selon le contexte. Compte tenu des capacités dynamiques du pianoforte, des nuances par paliers de *forte* et de *piano* sont stylistiquement adaptées, ainsi que des *crescendos* ou *decrescendos* occasionnels sur quelques notes. L'utilisation de la pédale est également possible, bien qu'encore une fois, cette utilisation doive rester discrète et modérée.

Franz Schubert
29. Écossaise op. 18 no 4 (D145)
(♩ = 80–84)
Cette *Écossaise* est aussi tumultueuse qu'elle est courte. Un son ferme, un toucher direct et une bonne base d'accords en soutien contribueront à bien faire sonner cette pièce.

30. Danse allemande D. 972 no 3
(♩ = 60–66)
Cette *Danse allemande* est probablement un peu plus complexe qu'elle n'y paraît, en particulier le passage de croches à la main droite. Vous pouvez appuyer le premier temps de chaque mesure en utilisant la pédale, soulignant ainsi subtilement le caractère dansant de l'œuvre. Le dernier temps de la mesure 12 constitue la levée de la mesure 13.

Daniel Steibelt
24. Cantabile en la mineur
(♩ = 42–46)
L'œuvre de Steibelt est un bon exemple de musique se situant à cheval sur la période classique et le romantisme. Sa ligne mélodique remarquable est particulièrement chantante et nécessite d'être mise en valeur, même lorsqu'elle passe à la main gauche comme aux mesures 17–20.

Johann Baptist Vanhal (1739–1813)
17. Sonatine op. 41 no 1
Arietta (♩ = 130–136), *Allegretto* (♩ = 152–156)
Cette œuvre de Vanhal est la première de sa série de *12 Sonatines faciles et progressives* op. 41. Hormis ses qualités musicales, la pièce présente de l'intérêt pour deux raisons bien spécifiques. Premièrement, elle s'ouvre sur un court prélude cadentiel qui installe la tonalité de do majeur, reflétant ainsi les pratiques musicales contemporaines de cette période. Deuxièmement, elle propose une sonatine complète sur une seule page, permettant aux élèves pianiste de ce niveau d'interpréter une pièce en deux mouvements. Par rapport à l'écriture musicale détaillée de ces derniers, la partie cadentielle ne contient que les notes, ce qui peut être compris comme une invitation à personnaliser la musique ou même à improviser autour du texte proposé, comme le faisaient sans doute les musiciens de cette époque.

Carl Maria von Weber
20. Allemande Op. 4 No. 9 (♩ = 132–138)
21. Allemande Op. 4 No. 2 (♩ = 140–144)

Les *Allemandes* de Weber sont tirées de son recueil de 12 allemandes op. 4. Dans le no 9 de cet opus, il vous faudra peut-être omettre le *sol* de la main gauche pendant deux temps afin de permettre à la note mélodique de la main droite d'être entendue. Aux mesures 7 et 15 du no 2, le pouce devra se placer sous les autres doigts lorsque vous commencerez le motif de croches afin d'être prêt à jouer la troisième croche de la mesure en temps utile.

Notes biographiques

Ludwig van Beethoven (1770–1827)
L'influence de Beethoven sur la musique de son temps ainsi que sur le développement des compositeurs de la génération suivante a été considérable et multiple. Son propre développement stylistique en tant que compositeur débouche sur un classement de sa production en trois périodes distinctes : jusqu'à environ 1802 (première période), de 1802 à 1812 (période intermédiaire) et à partir de 1812 (période tardive). En termes d'écriture pianistique, ces périodes reflètent l'héritage classique de la phase initiale, le développement de son style virtuose au clavier et l'individualité structurelle et technique qui en a découlé dans ses œuvres plus tardives.

En tant que compositeur, Beethoven excellait dans presque toutes les formes de musique instrumentale, du quatuor à cordes et de la sonate pour piano au concerto et à la symphonie. La spontanéité, la force et l'impact émotionnel de sa musique sont cependant le résultat d'un processus de composition méticuleux, documenté en détail grâce à ses carnets d'esquisses et ses manuscrits. Beethoven était un pianiste-interprète reconnu, bien que les témoignages contemporains sur sa façon de jouer diffèrent selon le point de vue de leur auteur. Tandis que certains louent sa puissance et la projection du son, d'autres trouvent son jeu brouillon et manquant de contrôle. Cependant, l'impact du jeu de Beethoven sur ses auditeurs est un point sur lequel la plupart des sources sont d'accord.

La fantaisie pour piano op. 77 est une œuvre pour piano où ces deux perspectives de son jeu sont réunies. Souvent considérée comme la version écrite d'une improvisation, elle contient de nombreux éléments caractéristiques de l'écriture de Beethoven du point de vue de l'harmonie, de la mélodie et de la texture, et en tant que telle, offre un aperçu unique des mécanismes d'écriture de ce grand musicien.

Les réalisations musicales de Beethoven sont si considérables que les générations suivantes de compositeurs, de Schubert à Schumann, Liszt et Brahms ont hésité un certain temps avant d'écrire dans un genre que Beethoven s'était approprié avant eux.

Johann Baptist Cramer (1771–1858)
Né en Allemagne, Cramer émigra en Angleterre à l'âge de trois ans avec sa famille. En 1783, il étudia pendant un an avec Muzio Clementi dont le style pianistique exerça sur lui une influence majeure lorsqu'il développa son propre style. Le *legato* de Cramer le rendit d'ailleurs célèbre parmi ses collègues et ses auditeurs. Comme Clementi avant lui, Cramer s'arrangea pour allier une carrière d'interprète, de professeur et d'homme d'affaires, s'impliquant dans l'édition musicale à partir de 1805. Ces rôles en apparence différents n'étaient pas rares parmi les musiciens de la seconde moitié du 18e siècle, en particulier dans la mesure où l'écriture et la publication de matériel pédagogique constituaient un marché relativement lucratif. Ses *84 Études pour le piano* (publiées en 1804 et 1810 en deux groupes de 42 études) étaient destinées à un public

d'élèves pianistes et furent autant un succès commercial qu'elles eurent d'influence d'un point de vue pianistique. Beethoven les recommandait pour le développement d'une bonne technique pianistique (il annota des études choisies de Cramer, mettant en valeur leurs objectifs musicaux individuels), Schumann les utilisa, Hanselt composa une seconde partie de piano pour l'y adjoindre et Carl Tausig (l'un des pianistes les plus célèbres du 19e siècle, élève de Liszt) édita une sélection de ces études soulignant ainsi leur pertinence presque un demi siècle après leur première publication.

Avant 1800, la vie de Cramer semble avoir consisté en leçons de piano et en tournées européennes. Après cette date, il resta essentiellement en Angleterre, se concentrant sur ses l'édition musicale et sur la composition. À son départ à la retraite en 1835, il était un membre hautement respecté de la vie musicale londonienne.

Anton Diabelli (1781–1858)
Actuellement, on se souvient du nom de Diabelli pour deux raisons principales : ses sonatines (et il y en a un certain nombre) et le thème sur lequel Beethoven fonda son grand cycle pour piano des *Variations Diabelli*, op. 120. Ces œuvres illustrent deux facettes des succès rencontré par Diabelli au cours de sa vie : celui d'un professeur d'instrument et d'un compositeur qui écrivait avec talent pour ses élèves, et celui de l'éditeur avisé qui invita 50 des compositeurs les plus renommés d'Autriche à lui fournir une variation à partir d'un thème de sa composition. Comme chacun le sait, Beethoven ne fournit pas ce qui lui était demandé, ni quand cela lui avait été demandé, mais produisit finalement un ensemble extraordinaire de variations d'une durée totale de cinquante-cinq minutes. La maison d'édition de Diabelli bâtit son succès en réalisant un équilibre entre l'édition de nombreuses œuvres commerciales et la défense des œuvres de Beethoven et Schubert, dont les premières œuvres imprimées furent éditées par Diabelli.

Johann Wilhelm Hässler (1747–1822)
Né à Erfurt en 1747, Hässler se forma auprès de son oncle, Johann Christian Kittel, organiste dans cette ville. À l'âge de 16 ans, il fut engagé pour la première fois en tant qu'organiste à Erfurt, mais commença bientôt à voyager dans toute l'Allemagne en tant que concertiste. Il fonda sa propre maison d'édition en 1780. En 1790, il avait voyagé aussi loin que l'Angleterre et la Russie, où il devint chef d'orchestre à la cour de Saint-Pétersbourg en 1792. Dans une lettre de 1788, le poète et écrivain Friedrich von Schiller se souvient des prestations de Hässler : « Il joue comme un maître et compose très bien. En tant que personne, c'est un original au tempérament plutôt fougueux. »[1] À partir de 1794, Hässler vécut à Moscou ou il exerça en tant que professeur de piano très respecté et recherché. Sa contribution au développement du pianisme russe au cours de la première moitié du 19e siècle reste à déterminer, mais la plupart de ses œuvres pour piano publiées suggèrent clairement qu'il s'intéressait au développement des capacités d'instrumentistes peu expérimentés.

Le style personnel de Hässler au clavier s'est développé à partir de l'écriture pianistique de C. P. E. Bach, mais partage son accessibilité avec les premières sonates pour piano de Haydn. Parmi ses petites pièces pédagogiques et ses sonates pour piano faciles, nombreuses sont celles qui bénéficient d'un attrait musical immédiat et sa méthode pour piano contient un grand nombre d'œuvres encore exploitables aujourd'hui.

1 Kahl, W., *Selbstbiographien Deutscher Musiker* (Koeln et Krefeld, Staufen Verlag, 1948), p.47

Tobias Haslinger (1787–1842)

Sa formation précoce de choriste à Linz permit à Haslinger d'apprendre différents instruments de musique. Après avoir emménagé à Vienne en 1810, il commença à éditer lui-même ses compositions avant de rejoindre la maison S.A. Steiner en tant qu'employé. Ses activités de compositeur (au total environ 100 œuvres partant de courtes pièces pour piano à deux messes) semblent de plus en plus avoir cédé le pas à ses intérêts d'éditeur. Son propre jugement musical ainsi que ses contacts personnels avec des compositeurs comme Beethoven et plus tard Johann Strauss et Liszt permirent à sa maison d'édition de prospérer. En 1826, il était propriétaire de la maison d'édition qui prit désormais son nom. Une annonce publicitaire de l'époque dénombre quelques 5000 titres musicaux figurant à son catalogue. Les succès commerciaux de Haslinger semblent avoir coïncidé avec la popularité croissante de la valse viennoise et le fait qu'il publiait deux de ses plus illustres représentants, Johann Strauss et Lanner.

Joseph Haydn (1732–1809)

L'estimation de la place de Haydn en tant que compositeur a été soumise à de nombreuses variations avec le temps. La perception populaire de sa vie se focalise souvent sur le relatif confort et la stabilité de ses presque 30 ans d'engagement auprès de la famille Esterhazy à Eisenstadt, près de Vienne. Malgré une existence effectivement relativement sédentaire (du moins par rapport à nombre de ses contemporains, et notamment à Mozart), la musique de Haydn fut largement publiée après 1780, lui permettant ainsi de jouir d'une réputation nationale et internationale croissante. À partir de 1791, ses visites à Londres vinrent confirmer ses succès économiques et musicaux.

Pourtant, ses premières années avaient été très différentes. Après une formation initiale de choriste et de violoniste, Haydn, qui n'était pas un virtuose, survécut en donnant des cours et en intégrant des ensembles jouant de la musique fonctionnelle. Du point de vue de la composition, essentiellement autodidacte, il progressa lentement jusqu'à acquérir les compétences nécessaires qui lui permirent, à partir du milieu des années 1760, de développer un style musical plus caractéristique.

La production pour piano de Haydn comprend plus de 60 sonates, pièces individuelles et variations. Bien que n'étant pas virtuose, il savait exactement comment écrire efficacement pour le pianoforte. Toutes ses œuvres viennent très bien sous les doigts (quel que soit leur degré de complexité), mais c'est l'élément de surprise, à la fois en termes d'harmonie et de texture pianistique, qui donne leur charme particulier à nombre de ses compositions. L'écriture pianistique de Haydn n'obéit jamais à des formules et garde ainsi toujours un caractère légèrement imprévisible.

Johann Nepomuk Hummel (1778–1837)

Hummel fut indubitablement une figure charnière de son époque, tant du point de vue pianistique que de l'écriture. La musique de Hummel, qui fut l'élève de Mozart, conserva toujours ses racines classiques en termes de structure et de détail musical. Cependant, en tant que pianiste, et plus important sans doute, en tant que professeur de piano influent, Hummel forma de nombreux représentants de la première génération du pianisme du 19e siècle : Henselt, Hiller, Mendelssohn et Thalberg ont tous bénéficié de son enseignement. D'autres pianistes de cette époque ont également subi son influence. Schumann envisagea d'étudier avec lui et si, pour finir, il ne le fit pas, les figurations décoratives de Hummel à la main droite l'occupèrent clairement, comme en témoignent les *Variations Abegg* op. 1 ainsi que d'autres œuvres de jeunesse. Liszt entra lui aussi en contact avec la musique de Hummel en jouant ses concertos pour piano op. 85 et 89 au début de sa carrière de virtuose itinérant. Même Chopin fut sans doute familier de la musique de Hummel, car certaines de ses premières œuvres dénotent des similitudes stylistiques et parfois même mélodiques.

La méthode de piano parue 1828, un document de 450 pages qui prétend mener l'élève « de la première leçon à la formation la plus complète »[1] constitue l'une des réalisations les plus remarquables de Hummel. Publiée à Vienne par Tobias Haslinger (voir morceau no 10 de la présente anthologie), il s'agit peut-être de la première méthode complète pour piano du 19e siècle établissant les concepts techniques sur lesquels se fonde l'art pianistique virtuose de cette période. Hormis la méthodologie d'apprentissage approfondie de Hummel, le caractère remarquable de cette méthode réside dans la conscience de son auteur de notions pédagogiques et de ses réflexions s'y rapportant : interaction maître-élève, motivation et déroulement du cours sont parmi les sujets explorés par Hummel.

August Eberhard Müller (1767–1817)

Müller semble avoir été un professeur-interprète-compositeur dont l'œuvre était très respectée de son temps. Pianiste, organiste et flûtiste de formation, il devint l'assistant de J.A. Hiller (1800) avant de lui succéder (1804) en tant que cantor à la Thomaskirche de Leipzig, poste occupé précédemment en particulier par J.S. Bach. En 1810, il fut engagé comme maître de chapelle à Weimar. En tant qu'auteur de répertoire pédagogique, Müller écrivit pour la flûte et pour le piano, avec un certain succès dans ce dernier cas. Bien que sa méthode de pianoforte de 1804 ait été une simple version mise à jour et augmentée de la *Pianoforteschule* de Loehlein, son succès est illustré par le fait qu'en 1825 Carl Czerny en supervisa la nouvelle édition et que le pianiste virtuose parisien Friedrich Kalkbrenner se servit du manuel de Müller comme base pour écrire le sien. Cela n'a donc rien de surprenant si des pièces individuelles de Müller continuèrent à circuler pendant la plus grande partie du 19e siècle. En tant qu'interprète, Müller jouait des œuvres de nombre de ses contemporains (notamment *La Création* de Hayden en 1801) et en tant qu'érudit, il rédigea un ouvrage sur l'interprétation des concertos de Mozart (1797).

Léopold Mozart (1719–1787)

Bien que sa réputation actuelle tienne surtout au fait qu'il fut le père de W.A. Mozart, Léopold Mozart fut un musicien distingué, compositeur et pédagogue à part entière. Après avoir commencé par étudier la philosophie, Mozart accorda toujours davantage d'importance à ses activités musicales. En vingt ans, il passa de premier violon (en quatrième position) à vice-maître de chapelle de l'orchestre à la cour de l'archevêque Léopold baron de Firmian, à Salzbourg. Il enseigna également le violon et les claviers, ce qui le mena ainsi en 1756 à la publication d'une méthode de violon très estimée. La capacité de Mozart à écrire de la musique pédagogique est particulièrement bien documentée grâce aux cahiers qu'il écrivit pour Nannerl et Wolfgang Amadeus, ses deux enfants. Sa production inclut de nombreuses symphonies, des sérénades, des concertos et des pièces pour le clavier, dont un grand nombre sont malheureusement considérées comme perdues. Parmi les pièces qui ont survécu, ses danses et petites œuvres pour claviers sont sans conteste les plus fréquemment jouées.

---

1 Hummel, J. N., *Anweisung zum Piano-forte spielen* (Vienne: Haslinger, 1828)

Wolfgang Amadeus Mozart (1756–1791)

Mozart naquit dans un environnement très musical. Son père Léopold était pédagogue et violoniste dans un orchestre à Salzbourg tandis que sa grande sœur, Nannerl, avait déjà révélé ses capacités au piano. Mozart fit des progrès rapides dans ses études musicales, à tel point que son père décida de l'emmener dans une tournée de concerts en l'Allemagne, puis à Londres et Paris. Ces voyages durèrent trois ans et demi avant que Mozart s'installe à Salzbourg en 1766. S'ensuivirent entre 1769 et 1772 des voyages annuels en Italie, qui permirent à Mozart d'entrer en contact avec de nombreux autres musiciens, comme il le fit tout au long de sa vie. Au début des années 1780, il semble que Mozart se soit établit comme musicien indépendant, avec tout ce que cela implique. Certains de ses concertos pour piano les plus célèbres datent de cette période, ainsi que nombre de ses quatuors à cordes dont il interpréta certain avec Joseph Haydn, leur dédicataire. À la fin de cette décennie (et au début de la suivante), Mozart rencontra un succès considérable comme compositeur d'opéra, avec des œuvres comme *Così fan tutte* et *La flûte enchantée*.

La diversité de ses œuvres pour piano reflète naturellement les différentes périodes de la vie du compositeur. Certaines parmi les plus précoces ont été écrites alors qu'il était à peine âgé de 5 ans, une époque où il écrivait principalement de courtes danses. Les œuvres de sa maturité incluent sonates, variations et pièces individuelles écrites le plus souvent à son usage personnel.

Franz Schubert (1797–1828)

La formation musicale initiale de Schubert lui a été prodiguée par son père et par ses frères qui lui enseignèrent le piano, le violon et l'alto. À l'âge de 11 ans, il bénéficia d'une bourse d'études qui lui permit de se former auprès de Salieri. Ensuite, à 16 ans, Schubert décida de se former à l'enseignement et commença un an plus tard à travailler dans l'école de son père. À 17 ans, il avait écrit certains de ses premiers chefs-d'œuvre, dont *Le Roi des aulnes* et *Marguerite au rouet*, pour voix et piano. En 1816, Schubert abandonna son poste d'enseignant et choisit de vivre au centre de Vienne et de se consacrer à la composition. S'ensuivit une période d'incertitude financière, mais à la fin de 1819, Schubert écrivit son premier chef-d'œuvre de musique de chambre, son quintette intitulé *La Truite*. Au printemps 1821, le succès du *Roi des aulnes* déboucha sur la publication de ses airs par Diabelli, qui lui permit de connaître une courte période de stabilité financière. De 1820 à 1823, il se lança dans l'écriture de musique d'opéra, une entreprise malheureusement peu fructueuse, pour finalement se tourner vers l'écriture de musique de chambre et de musique symphonique les trois dernières années de ma vie. À quelques rares exceptions près, l'écriture pianistique de Schubert ne se préoccupe pas d'effets techniques tels que le font certains de ses contemporains. Au contraire, toutes les exigences de sa musique proviennent de la prééminence du propos musical sur toute autre forme d'affichage pianistique.

Daniel Steibelt (1765–1823)

La vie de Steibelt reflète pour une grande part les conditions vécues par de nombreux interprètes compositeurs de cette époque. Né dans un pays, mais vivant et travaillant dans de nombreux autres pays, Steibelt, à l'instar de Hässler et Field, finit par s'installer en Russie. Cependant, sa personnalité et ses affaires peuvent en elles-mêmes avoir nécessité des changements relativement réguliers d'environnement ! Ses contemporains rapportent en effet un caractère extravagant et vaniteux, ainsi qu'un penchant pour l'escroquerie. Dettes non honorées et ruptures de contrats confèrent à Steibelt une réputation pittoresque, de même que sa propension à vendre comme étant nouvelles des œuvres préexistantes à peine remaniées (la plupart du temps les siennes propres). Le fait que Steibelt fut un bon pianiste est rarement remis en question, mais du point de vue de l'écriture, ses compositions répondent généralement à une demande de musique à la mode du moment. Steibelt était manifestement à l'aise dans le genre des courtes pièces de caractère pour piano, qu'il s'agisse de préludes ou d'études. De par leur contenu musical en grande partie marqué par l'invention pianistique et leur présentation dans un format relativement condensé, les miniatures de Steibelt peuvent produire un effet inhabituellement marquant. Sa *Méthode* pour le piano de 1805 ainsi que ses *50 études* op. 78 constituent un répertoire particulièrement intéressant pour les apprentis pianistes et leurs professeurs.

Johann Baptist Vanhal (1739–1813)

Originaire de Bohème, le compositeur Vanhal bénéficia d'une formation de chanteur et de violoniste (plus tard également au clavier) avant de s'installer à Vienne à l'âge de 21 ans. Il y travailla en tant qu'enseignant dans le privé où il eut notamment pour élève le jeune Ignace Pleyel. En 1769, il partit pour une tournée de deux ans en Italie avant de revenir à Vienne. En tant que compositeur, Vanhal s'intéressa à différents genres selon les époques. Il se détourna de l'écriture symphonique en 1780, puis, quelques années plus tard, cessa d'écrire des quatuors à cordes, se concentrant alors plutôt sur la musique pour clavier et la musique sacrée. Les proportions dans lesquelles ses œuvres furent publiées de son vivant l'établissent comme une figure musicale d'importance, alors même que nombre d'entre elles sont restées à l'état de manuscrit. Ainsi une perspective complète de son œuvre est toujours en attente de réalisation.

Carl Maria von Weber (1786–1826)

La première partie de la vie de Weber est emblématique de celle de nombreux musiciens de son temps. Son éducation musicale lui fut prodiguée par son père et par plusieurs musiciens locaux. Ses voyages en Allemagne et en Autriche lui permirent ensuite de rencontrer Michael Haydn (frère de Joseph et compositeur très reconnu) ainsi que le compositeur et théoricien Georg Joseph Vogler qui lui dispensa une grande partie de l'enseignement systématique dont il avait besoin. Weber déménagea de ville en ville jusqu'en 1810, occupant successivement différents de postes musicaux, voire dans certains cas, administratifs. Une action en justice contre Weber et son père ainsi que leur arrestation et, pour finir, leur bannissement du land du Wurtemberg, eurent sur lui un profond retentissement. Déterminé à changer de vie, il passa les deux années suivantes à composer, donner des concerts et à vivre à la hauteur de ses moyens. Il fut bientôt engagé en tant que directeur musical à la cour et/ou au théâtre, d'abord à Prague entre 1813 et 1816 puis à Dresde entre 1817 et 1821, périodes au cours desquelles il continua également à voyager en tant qu'interprète. Le changement sans doute le plus important dans la vie de Weber fut provoqué par l'extraordinaire popularité de son opéra, *Der Freischütz* (1820), une œuvre qui assura son succès dans toute l'Allemagne ainsi qu'à l'étranger.

L'écriture pianistique de Weber est caractéristique, mais reste cependant difficile à résumer. Elle est clairement dominée par la mélodie, dans la mesure où elle est souvent homophonique, avec une attirance particulière pour les formes de danses et les motifs rythmiques pointés qui sous-tendent son style de composition. En tant que pianiste, Weber écrit souvent de manière élaborée et virtuose pour la main droite : des progressions d'accords rapides, des croisements de mains et des extensions dépassant largement la position d'une main. En ce sens, l'écriture pour piano de Weber est fondée sur la technique fluide de gammes et d'arpèges également privilégiée par Hummel, mais il occupe une position intermédiaire entre ce dernier et le discours pianistique de Chopin et Liszt à partir des années 1830.

Spielhinweise

Eine der interessanten Herausforderungen beim Spielen klassischer Musik ist der Umgang mit dem Unterschied zwischen dem Pianoforte des späten 18. Jahrhunderts und dem heutigen Klavier. Die Unterschiede sind zwar recht groß, doch können eingebrachte Kenntnisse über die damaligen Instrumente unseren Umgang mit der Musik bereichern, auch wenn wir sie auf modernen Instrumenten spielen. So hatte das Klavier der Klassik leichtere (und weniger) Tasten, die Saiten verliefen parallel zueinander, d.h. es gab keine kreuzsaitige Bespannung, die Hämmer waren nicht mit Filz, sondern mit Leder bezogen, es war insgesamt zierlicher, hatte keinen Metallrahmen und eine andere Mechanik. All das bedeutet, dass wir den Klang, den Haydn oder Mozart hörten, nicht reproduzieren können. Wir können das moderne Klavier jedoch so spielen, dass es diesen anderen musikalischen Gegebenheiten gerecht wird. Um dies zu erreichen, sollte man mit starken dynamischen Kontrasten zwischen *forte* und *piano* arbeiten und das rechte Pedal so einsetzen, dass es nur bestimmte Stellen der Musik hervorhebt und nicht allgegenwärtig ist. Die Klangqualität sollte sich grundsätzlich eher an den Höhen als an den Bässen des Instruments orientieren. Verzierungen sind ebenfalls wichtig, und die CD enthält ab und zu Verzierungen an den Stellen mit Kadenzen. Die Verwendung von Verzierungen ist häufig eine Frage der persönlichen Entscheidung. Am besten betrachtet man Verzierungen als subtile Bereicherung einer Melodie.

Letztendlich bildet das Konzept der historisch geprägten Spielpraxis (d.h. ein Verständnis dafür, wie Musik in einer anderen Epoche gespielt wurde sowie der Einfluss auf das eigene Spiel) eine hervorragende Grundlage für das Experimentieren mit Musik sowie für das Zuhören, Bewerten und Treffen von Entscheidungen.

Ludwig van Beethoven

11. Deutscher Tanz WoO 42 Nr. 1
(♩ = 152–160)

Diese *Allemande* wurde Mitte der 1790er-Jahre komponiert und 1814 als eine von sechs Allemanden für Klavier und Geige veröffentlicht. Die Version für Soloklavier erschien erstmals 1855, und möglicherweise erfolgte die Bearbeitung (die im Wesentlichen aus dem Weglassen der Geigenstimme besteht) durch den Herausgeber W. Plachy. Die größte Herausforderung des Stückes ist, die Viertel mit der rechten und die Achtel mit der linken Hand gleichzeitig zu spielen. Die Finger sollten immer dicht über den Tasten liegen, vor allem die der linken Hand, damit beide Hände gut aufeinander abgestimmt werden können. Eine leichte Betonung der Eins trägt dazu bei, das Gefühl eines Tanzes im 3/4-Takt zu vermitteln.

12. Ecossaise WoO 86
(♩ = 152–160)

Beethovens Manuskript ist auf den 14. November 1825 datiert und gehört somit zum Spätwerk des Komponisten. Im Original gibt es zwar keine Tempoangabe, doch werden durch das musikalische Gefühl von einem betonten Schlag pro Takt einige Tempo-Parameter festgelegt. Wie so oft bei Kompositionen für eine Sammlung enthält der Autograph zwar einige, aber nicht alle Artikulationsangaben. Die gepunkteten Linien stammen vom Herausgeber und müssen somit nicht unbedingt beachtet werden. Einige Koordinationsaspekte in Bezug auf Akkorde und einzelne Noten für beide Hände erfordern eine sorgfältige Vorbereitung,

da die rechte Hand in der Tonart Es-Dur Positionen einnehmen muss, in denen der Daumen manchmal weiße und manchmal schwarze Tasten spielt. Solche Handbewegungen sind eine gute Vorbereitung für zukünftige Spielstücke, in denen diese Fähigkeiten erforderlich sind.

28. Ecossaise WoO 23
(♩ = 118–124)

Das Werk erschien 1810 in einer Publikation, die sich *Musikalisches Pfennigmagazin* nannte: eine Sammlung sehr kurzer Miniaturen von namhaften und anonymen Komponisten zu einem sehr günstigen Preis. Beethovens lebhafter Schottischer Tanz besteht aus drei Teilen, wobei der erste und dritte Teil identisch sind. Die Oktavsprünge in der linken Hand (Takt 9–12) sollten ganz gleichmäßig, aber trotzdem *staccato* gespielt werden. Takt 13 und 14 enthalten Akzente auf unbetonten Zählzeiten, die den Rhythmus der Melodiestimme in Takt 3 und 4 widerspiegeln. Um Sicherheit in der linken Hand zu entwickeln, kann man die Noten der Anfangstakte für die linke Hand als Akkorde üben, bevor man das Stück wie notiert spielt:

Johann Baptist Cramer

19. Allegretto in C-Dur
(♩. = 72–76)

Sowohl dieses als auch das nächste Stück von Cramer stammt aus der „Schulausgabe", d.h. einer gekürzten Version seiner Klavierschule. Cramer nannte es – „Anweisung das Piano-Forte zu spielen, oder deutlicher Unterricht in den Anfangsgründen der Musik, die vorzüglichsten Regeln des Fingersatzes, in vielen und gewählten Beispielen, nebst 41 Lectionen und Vorspielen in den gebräuchlichsten Dur- und Molltonarten". [1]

Der Fingersatz in diesem Stück stammt vom Komponisten. Das Werk wirkt wie eine kurze Etüde, ein Stück, das gut klingen und den Interpreten an eine bestimmte Fähigkeit heranführen soll. Bei diesem *Allegretto* scheint die gleichmäßige Sechzehntelpassage das Wichtigste zu sein. Einmal erlernt, kann das Werk für viele verschiedene Zwecke verwendet werden, z.B. zum Einspielen oder als Grundlage für Transponierexperimente.

25. Präludium & Air Russe
(♩ = 116–120), (♩ = 96–104)

Präludium & Air Russe stammt aus derselben Publikation wie das obige *Allegretto* und verfolgt dasselbe Konzept, das auch in Vanhals *Sonatine* op. 41 Nr. 1 in diesem Band (Stück Nr. 17) zu finden ist. Im späten 18. und frühen 19. Jahrhundert war es üblich, dass Pianisten ihr Publikum auf das jeweilige Stück vorbereiteten, meist durch eine kurze Einleitung oder Improvisation in der Tonart des Stückes. Das vorliegende *Präludium* verfolgt genau diesen Zweck. Man kann die zugrunde liegende Moll-Akkordfolge des Präludiums hören, wenn man jede Triolengruppe als Viertelakkord spielt. *Air Russe* ist Cramers Version eines russischen Liedes, das damals als *Schöne Minka* bekannt war. Es wurde auch von Weber als Thema

---

1 Cramer, J. B., *Anweisung das Piano-Forte zu spielen* (Offenbach : Johann André, Nr. 3661, ohne Datum)

für seine Variationen op. 40 (1815) und von Beethoven in seinen Volksliedvariationen op. 107 (1820) verwendet. Cramers Version ist eine nützliche Übung, um Sexten mit und ohne Pedaleinsatz zu spielen.

Anton Diabelli
4. Klavierstück op. 125 Nr. 7
(♩. = 120–124)
Das Training für die linke Hand zur Vorbereitung von Akkordwechseln ist ein wichtiger Bestandteil beim Erlernen dieses Stückes. Zu diesem Zweck kann man alle Noten für die linke Hand als Akkord (einen pro Takt) und dazu die rechte Hand wie notiert spielen. Wenn das gut klappt, trennt man die Töne für die linke Hand wie notiert. Die Artikulation der rechten Hand ist weitgehend unkompliziert, bis auf die wiederkehrende Figur in Takt 3:

Wenn man sich die Notation folgendermaßen vorstellt, klingt es richtig:

5. Klavierstück op. 125 Nr. 6
(♩. = 112–116)
Die linke Hand spielt in Takt 1, 2, 13 und 14 gehaltene Töne in der Unterstimme und wechselnde Töne in der Oberstimme. Um diese Koordinationsfähigkeit zu entwickeln, sollte man Folgendes ein paar Mal üben, bevor man die Takte wie notiert spielt:

Johann Wilhelm Häßler
23. Ecossaise in G-Dur
(♩ = 118–124)
Dieses Stück ist mit seiner eingängigen Melodie und dem straffen Rhythmus hervorragend als Vortragsstück geeignet. Damit der Rhythmus zur Geltung kommt, sollten die Achtel (die auf den Zählzeiten liegen) und nicht die jeweils erste Sechzehntel betont werden. Außerdem klingen dadurch die Gruppen aus drei gebundenen Noten gleichmäßiger. Um die Terzen in Takt 9–12 möglichst gleichmäßiger zu spielen, sollte man sie langsam als wiederholte Sechzehntel anstatt als einzelne Achtel üben. Schließlich sollte man beim langsamen Üben den Unterschied zwischen *legato* und *staccato* gespielten Tönen übertreiben, damit das Publikum den Unterschied zwischen gebundenen und abgestoßenen Tönen auch dann noch hört, wenn das Stück im normalen Tempo gespielt wird.

Tobias Haslinger
10. Sonatina in C-Dur
(♩ = 108–116)
Wie Häßlers *Eccosaise* erfordert die *Sonatina* einen Kontrast zwischen *legato* und *staccato* gespielten Tönen. Die musikalische Artikulation sollte bereits ab den allerersten Lernstadien einbezogen werden, da sie ein wesentlicher Bestandteil des Stückes ist. Um die Achtel in Takt 11 ganz gleichmäßig zu spielen, vor allem beim Überkreuzen mit dem dritten Finger, sollte der Ellenbogen leicht nach außen gedreht werden, um den Übersatz mit dem dritten Finger zu unterstützen.

Joseph Haydn
8. Deutscher Tanz Hob. IX: 8
(♩ = 152–156)
Diese Allemande muss nicht schnell gespielt werden, vor allem, da der Unterschied zwischen gebundenen und ungebundenen Tönen sehr deutlich sein muss. Um dies zu erreichen, ist ein Blick auf den Fingersatz in Takt 2–3 hilfreich. Es mag zwar unkonventionell sein, den dritten Finger für aufeinander folgende Achtel über den Taktstrich hinweg zu verwenden, doch trägt dies zur Betonung des von Haydn notierten Legatos bei. Wenn man sich für diesen Fingersatz entscheidet, sollte das C ganz leicht und kurz klingen, und der dritte Finger sollte die Tasten beim Wechsel zum H kaum verlassen. Geht es auch einfacher? Man kann den Fingersatz in den Klammern ausprobieren. Letzten Endes bestimmt der Klang der Melodiestimme, wie man diese Stelle spielen möchte.

15. Deutscher Tanz Hob. IX: 12
(♩ = 66–72)
Wenn die Finger beim Spielen der ersten Achtel jeder Gruppe (d.h. jedes Takts) fast alle Achtel des Takts abdecken, kann man diesen Tanz schon bald recht schnell spielen.

22. Kontretanz Hob. XXXIc: 17b
(♩ = 60–66)
Dieser Tanz entstand in London und ist die Klavierversion eines Stückes, das ursprünglich für ein größeres Ensemble geschrieben wurde. Beim vorgeschlagenen Fingersatz in Takt 3 werden zwei Achtel gebunden. Wenn man dies ändern möchte, muss man auch den Fingersatz ändern.

Johann Nepomuk Hummel
9. Ecossaise op. 52 Nr. 5
(♩ = 160–164)
Dies ist mit Abstand das kürzeste Stück der Sammlung aus sechs leichten Stücken op. 52. Seit ihrer Veröffentlichung ist die Ecossaise Bestandteil zahlreicher Klavierschulen. Der Kontrast zwischen dem *piano* der ersten und dem *fortissimo*-Beginn der zweiten Zeile sollte stark hervorgehoben werden. Hier kann man richtig in die Tasten greifen! Die Bassstimme im zweiten Teil erfordert vielleicht etwas zusätzliche Aufmerksamkeit. Hier kann es nützlich sein, die Unterstimme zu halten und gleichzeitig die Achtel *staccato* zu üben. Das ist zwar schwieriger, doch ist das Resultat überzeugender, wenn man beide Zeilen wieder *legato* spielt.

26. Un poco adagio (Air Russe)
(♩ = 60–66)
Dieses Stück ist zwar sehr kurz, hat aber eine sehr schöne Melodie. Die Schwerpunkte liegen auf dem Legatospiel und darauf,

dass jede der drei Stimmen beim Übergang von einem Ton zum nächsten gut zu hören ist.

August Eberhard Müller

27. Siciliano in g-Moll
(♩. = 52–56)

Das Stück stammt aus „Müllers Sammlung" Instructive Übungsstücke für das Pianoforte, einer der damals führenden Klavierschulen. Das Werk scheint in zwei Versionen in a- und g-Moll zu existieren. Abgesehen von den etwas merkwürdigen Dynamikangaben lässt die Notation dem Pianisten viel Interpretationsspielraum.

Leopold Mozart

1. Menuett in d-Moll
(♩ = 144–152)

Die Noten enthalten keine dynamischen oder Artikulationszeichen, sodass der Interpret das Werk nach seinem eigenen musikalischen Geschmack gestalten kann. Auf der CD-Aufnahme spiele ich die Achtel *legato*, doch ist dies lediglich eine Option. Man könnte die Achtel auch in Zweiergruppen binden, vor allem, wenn man das Stück etwas langsamer spielen möchte. Was auch immer dabei herauskommen mag: Der interessante Aspekt beim Erlernen dieses Stückes ist die Möglichkeit zu experimentieren und anschließend Entscheidungen zu treffen.

2. Menuett in F-Dur
(♩ = 156–162)

Auch hier lässt die Partitur viele Möglichkeiten offen, in Bezug auf Artikulation und Dynamik zu experimentieren und Entscheidungen treffen. Um die Eins im Takt zu betonen, spiele ich die Eins und Zwei in Takt 1, 3 und 5 gebunden.

7. Menuett in C-Dur
(♩ = 132–136)

Wie die beiden vorherigen Stücke stammt auch dieses Werk aus Leopold Mozarts *Notenbuch* von 1759 und wurde für seine Tochter Nannerl geschrieben. Um den Unterschied zwischen Sechzehnteln und Triolen in diesem Stück zu verdeutlichen, sollte der Rhythmus zwischen punktierter Achtel und Sechzehntel verstärkt werden, indem man Letztere ein kleines bisschen verzögert.

18. Bourée in e-Moll
(♩ = 70–76)

Für diese *Bourée* gibt es mehrere Ansätze. Man kann alle Viertel etwas ungebunden und alle Achtelgruppen paarweise gebunden spielen. Man kann aber auch einige Viertelgruppen überbinden. Wenn dies mit dem Grundrhythmus des Stückes im Einklang steht, ist es ebenfalls eine gute Lösung.

Wolfgang Amadeus Mozart

3. Minuet KV 6 / IIIa (♩ = 136–140)
6. Minuet KV 1e (♩ = 120–128)
13. Allegro KV3 (♩ = 60–66)
14. Minuet KV5 (♩ = 120–126)
16. Minuet KV2 (♩. = 50–56)

Diese Stücke gehören zu Mozarts frühesten Kompositionen und entstanden höchstwahrscheinlich unter der Aufsicht seines Vaters Leopold. Meist enthalten die Stücke kaum Spielanweisungen, so dass es dem Interpreten überlassen bleibt, einen dynamischen Rahmen sowie die passende Artikulation zu wählen. Generell ist

es wahrscheinlich angemessen, alle längeren Töne voneinander zu trennen, wenn sie nicht unbedingt gebunden gespielt werden sollten. Achtel können je nach Kontext in Zweier- oder Dreiergruppen gebunden werden. Angesichts des dynamischen Umfangs der frühen Pianofortes steht die Terrassendynamik von *forte* und *piano* sowie ein gelegentliches *crescendo* oder *decrescendo* über einigen Tönen im Einklang mit dem damaligen Stil. Der Einsatz des Pedals ist ebenfalls möglich, obgleich man auch damit sparsam umgehen sollte.

Franz Schubert

29. Ecossaise op. 18 Nr. 4 (D145)
(♩ = 80–84)

Diese *Ecossaise* ist kurz und spritzig. Ein fester Klang, ein direkter Anschlag und unterstützende Grundakkorde tragen dazu bei, dass dieses Stück eindrucksvoll klingt.

30. Deutscher Tanz D. 972 Nr. 3
(♩ = 60–66)

Der *Deutsche Tanz* ist wahrscheinlich etwas schwieriger als er klingt, vor allem die Achtelpassagen für die rechte Hand. Man kann die Eins in jedem Takt mithilfe des Pedals hervorheben, was das Tänzerische des Werks geschickt unterstreicht. Der letzte Schlag in Takt 12 sollte als Auftakt zu Takt 13 dienen.

Daniel Steibelt (1765–1823)

24. Cantabile in a-Moll
(♩ = 42–46)

Steibelts Werk ist ein schönes Beispiel für die Musik, die in der Übergangzeit von der Klassik zur Romantik entstand. Die Melodiestimme hat Vokalcharakter und muss hervorgehoben werden, auch wenn sie in Takt 17–20 mit der linken Hand gespielt wird.

Johann Baptist Vanhal (1739–1813)

17. Sonatina op. 41 Nr. 1
Arietta (♩ = 130–136), *Allegretto* (♩ = 152–156)

Vanhals Werk ist das erste einer Reihe von *12 Sonatinas faciles et progressives* op. 41. Abgesehen von seinen musikalischen Qualitäten ist das Stück aus zwei Gründen interessant. Erstens beginnt es mit einer kurzen Kadenz als Einleitung, in der die Tonart C-Dur eingeführt wird, was die damalige Aufführungspraxis widerspiegelt. Zweitens bietet es eine komplette Sonatine auf einer Seite und ermöglicht es Schülern dieser Spielstufe, ein Werk in zwei Sätzen zu spielen. Im Vergleich zu den musikalischen Details der zwei Sätze enthält der Kadenzteil lediglich die Noten, was als Aufforderung zur individuellen Interpretation der Musik oder sogar zur Improvisation verstanden werden kann, eine damals durchaus übliche Praxis.

Carl Maria von Weber

20. Allemande op. 4 Nr. 9 (♩ = 132–138)
21. Allemande op. 4 Nr. 2 (♩ = 140–144)

Webers Allemanden stammen aus der Sammlung *12 Allemanden* op. 4. In Nr. 9 muss man vielleicht das g in der linken Hand zwei Schläge lang weglassen, damit der Melodieton der rechten Hand zu hören ist. In Nr. 2 sollte der Daumen in Takt 7 und 15 unter den anderen Fingern warten, wenn man mit dem Achtellauf beginnt und somit bereit sein, die dritte Achtel im Takt zu spielen.

Biografische Anmerkungen

Ludwig van Beethoven (1770–1827)

Beethovens Einfluss auf die musikalische Richtung seiner Zeit sowie auf die musikalische Entwicklung nachfolgender Komponisten war beträchtlich und vielschichtig. Seine eigene stilistische Entwicklung als Komponist lässt sich in drei verschiedene Zeitabschnitte einteilen: bis ca. 1802 (erste Schaffensperiode), von 1802 bis 1812 (zweite Schaffensperiode) und ab 1812 (dritte Schaffensperiode). Hinsichtlich Beethovens Klavierkompositionen reflektieren diese Perioden das klassische Erbe seiner Anfangsphase, die Entwicklung seines virtuosen Spielstils und die darauf folgende Individualität seiner späteren Werke in Bezug auf Technik und Aufbau.

Als Komponist zeichnete sich Beethoven in fast allen Formen der Instrumentalmusik aus, von Streichquartetten über Klaviersonaten und Konzerte bis zu Sinfonien. Die Spontaneität, Stärke und emotionale Wirkung seiner Musik waren jedoch das Ergebnis eines akribisch gestalteten Kompositionsprozesses, den er in seinen Skizzenbüchern und Autographen dokumentierte. Beethoven war ein erfolgreicher Pianist, obgleich seine Leistung in zeitgenössischen Berichten je nach Schwerpunkt des Autors unterschiedlich bewertet wurde. Während einige Beethovens kraftvollen Klang lobten, fanden andere sein Spiel chaotisch und unkontrolliert. Die meisten Quellen sind sich jedoch über die Wirkung einig, die Beethoven mit seinem Spiel auf sein Publikum ausübte.

Ein Klavierwerk, das beide Sichtweisen seines Spiels vereint, ist die Fantasie für Klavier op. 77, ein Werk, das weithin als niedergeschriebene Version einer Improvisation angesehen wird. Es enthält viele für Beethoven typische Aspekte hinsichtlich Harmonik, Melodie und Aufbau und bietet daher einen einzigartigen Einblick in das Schaffen des großen Musikers.

Beethovens kompositorische Leistungen waren so beachtlich, dass nachfolgende Komponistengenerationen von Schubert bis Schumann, Liszt und Brahms einige Zeit zögerten, bevor sie in einem Genre komponierten, das Beethoven sich zuvor zu eigen gemacht hatte.

Johann Baptist Cramer (1771–1858)

Cramer wurde in Deutschland geboren und zog im Alter von drei Jahren mit seiner Familie nach England. 1783 nahm er ein Jahr lang Unterricht bei Muzio Clementi, dessen Klavierstil Cramer in der Entwicklung seines eigenen Stils prägte. Cramer war bei seinen Kollegen und seinem Publikum für seinen Legato-Anschlag bekannt. Wie Clementi zuvor schaffte es Cramer, eine Karriere als Pianist, Lehrer und musikalischer Unternehmer zu kombinieren und war ab 1805 auch als Musikverleger tätig. Diese scheinbar so unterschiedlichen Rollen waren bei den Musikern der zweiten Hälfte des 18. Jahrhunderts durchaus üblich, vor allem, da insbesondere das Verfassen und Veröffentlichen von Unterrichtsmaterial einen lukrativen Markt darstellte. Cramers *84 Etüden* für Klavier (1804 und 1810 in zwei Teilen à 42 Etüden erschienen), die sich an ein breites Publikum richteten, waren sowohl kommerziell erfolgreich als auch ausgesprochen einflussreich, was klavierspielerische Aspekte anging. Beethoven empfahl sie zur Entwicklung der Klavierspieltechnik (er kommentierte ausgewählte Cramer-Etüden und hob deren jeweilige musikalische Ziele hervor), Schumann verwendete sie, Henselt komponierte eine zweite Klavierstimme dazu, und der Liszt-Schüler Carl Tausig (einer der meistgefeierten Pianisten des 19. Jahrhunderts) gab eine Auswahl von Cramer-Etüden heraus und unterstrich somit ein halbes Jahrhundert nach

deren Erstveröffentlichung ihre Bedeutung.

Cramers Leben vor 1800 bestand hauptsächlich aus Klavierunterricht und Konzertreisen durch ganz Europa. Nach 1800 hielt er sich hauptsächlich in England auf und konzentrierte sich auf seinen Verlag und das Komponieren. Cramer setzte sich 1835 als hoch angesehenes Mitglied der Londoner Musikszene zur Ruhe.

Anton Diabelli (1781–1858)

Heute bringt man Diabellis Namen hauptsächlich mit zwei Dingen in Verbindung: mit Sonatinen (von denen es einige gibt) und mit der Vorlage, die er Beethoven für seinen umfangreichsten Klavierzyklus, die Diabelli-Variationen op. 120, lieferte. Diese Werke markieren zwei erfolgreiche Abschnitte in Diabellis Leben: den des komponierenden Instrumentallehrers, der ansprechende Unterrichtswerke schrieb, und den des cleveren Musikverlegers, der 50 der renommiertesten österreichischen Komponisten bat, ihm eine Variation über ein von ihm selbst komponiertes Thema zu liefern. Beethoven lieferte bekanntlich nicht das, worum er gebeten worden war, und auch nicht zum gewünschten Zeitpunkt, sondern schrieb ein 55-minütiges Werk mit verschiedenen Variationen.

Diabellis Erfolg als Verleger gründete sich auf dem Gleichgewicht zwischen der Veröffentlichung zahlreicher kommerzieller Werke und dem Einsatz für die Musik von Beethoven und Schubert, deren früheste Druckwerke von Diabelli veröffentlicht wurden.

Johann Wilhelm Häßler (1747–1822)

Häßler wurde 1747 in Erfurt geboren und erhielt von seinem Onkel, dem Erfurter Organisten Johann Christian Kittel, eine musikalische Ausbildung. Im Alter von 16 Jahren spielte Häßler zum ersten Mal als Organist in Erfurt, unternahm jedoch schon bald darauf Konzertreisen durch Deutschland. 1780 gründete er einen eigenen Musikverlag und reiste bis 1790 u. a. nach England und Russland, wo er 1792 Hofkapellmeister in St. Petersburg wurde. In einem Brief von 1788 erinnert sich der Dichter und Schriftsteller Friedrich von Schiller an Häßlers Klavierspiel: „Er spielte meisterhaft. Er komponiert selbst sehr gut. Der Mensch hat viel Originelles und überaus viel Feuer". [1]

Ab 1794 lebte Häßler in Moskau, wo er als hoch angesehener und gefragter Klavierlehrer arbeitete. Sein Beitrag zur Entwicklung des russischen Klavierspiels in der ersten Hälfte des 19. Jahrhunderts ist zwar noch nicht ganz klar, doch geben die meisten seiner veröffentlichten Werke für Klavier Aufschluss darüber, dass er sich auf die Entwicklung der Fähigkeiten weniger erfahrener Pianisten konzentrierte.

Häßler entwickelte seinen eigenen Klavierstil nach dem Vorbild der Klavierwerke von C. P. E. Bach, doch waren seine Werke ebenso zugänglich wie Haydns frühe Klaviersonaten. Viele von Häßlers kürzeren Unterrichtsstücken und leichten Klaviersonaten profitieren von ihrer unmittelbaren musikalischen Anziehungskraft, und seine Klavierschule enthält zahlreiche Werke, die auch heute noch Verwendung finden.

Tobias Haslinger (1787–1842)

Aufgrund seiner frühen Ausbildung als Chorknabe in Linz konnte Haslinger mehrere Instrumente erlernen. Nach seinem Umzug nach Wien im Jahr 1810 veröffentlichte er einige seiner Werke im Eigenverlag, bevor er im Musikverlag S.A. Stainer arbeitete. Seine Aktivitäten als Komponist (insgesamt ca. 100 Werke, von kürzeren Klavierstücken bis zu zwei Messen) machten zunehmend seinen unternehmerischen Interessen Platz. Haslingers musikalisches Ur-

1 Kahl, W., *Selbstbiographien Deutscher Musiker* (Koeln und Krefeld, Staufen Verlag, 1948), p.47

teil und sein persönlicher Kontakt zu Komponisten wie Beethoven und später Johann Strauß und Liszt verhalfen seinem Verlag zu großem Erfolg. Ab 1826 gehörte ihm das Unternehmen, das fortan seinen Namen trug. In einer damaligen Anzeige waren 5.000 musikalische Werke als Teil seines Verlagsprogramms verzeichnet. Haslingers Geschäftserfolg ist wohl nicht zuletzt der wachsenden Popularität des Wiener Walzers und der Veröffentlichung der Werke zweier seiner berühmtesten Vertreter, Johann Strauß und Lanner zu verdanken.

Joseph Haydn (1732–1809)

Die Bewertung von Haydns Stellung als Komponist hat sich im Laufe der Zeit immer wieder verändert. Zahlreiche Berichte konzentrieren sich auf die Sicherheit und Stabilität seiner fast 30-jährigen Anstellung bei der Familie Esterhazy in Eisenstadt bei Wien. Trotz dieses verhältnismäßig beständigen Lebens (zumindest im Vergleich zu vielen seiner Zeitgenossen, nicht zuletzt Mozart) wurde Haydns Musik ab 1780 veröffentlicht und erfreute sich zunehmender Beliebtheit, was dem Komponisten wachsende nationale und internationale Bedeutung einbrachte. Seine Besuche in London ab 1791 untermauerten seine musikalischen und wirtschaftlichen Erfolge.

Seine frühen Jahre sahen jedoch völlig anders aus. Nach seiner Ausbildung als Chorsänger und Violinist hielt sich Haydn, der kein virtuoser Musiker war, mit Unterricht und als Mitglied wechselnder Ensembles, die bei Veranstaltungen musizierten, über Wasser. Als Komponist eignete sich Haydn als Autodidakt nur langsam die notwendigen Fähigkeiten an. Ab Mitte der 1760er-Jahre entwickelte er dann allmählich seinen eigenen Musikstil.

Haydns Klavierwerke umfassen 60 Sonaten, Einzelstücke und Variationen. Obwohl er kein Klaviervirtuose war, wusste er genau, worauf es bei einer Komposition für das Pianoforte ankam. All seine Werke lassen sich sehr gut spielen (ungeachtet ihrer verschiedenen Schwierigkeitsgrade), doch ist das Überraschungsmoment, das sich sowohl in der Harmonik als auch im Aufbau ausdrücken kann, letztendlich für den besonderen Charme vieler Stücke verantwortlich. Haydns Klavierkompositionen sind niemals starr und daher immer unvorhersehbar.

Johann Nepomuk Hummel (1778–1837)

Der Mozartschüler Hummel war zu Lebzeiten eine Schlüsselfigur. Seine Musik blieb sowohl hinsichtlich ihres Aufbaus als auch der musikalischen Details immer ihren klassischen Wurzeln treu. Als Pianist und, was vielleicht am wichtigsten ist, als einflussreicher Klavierlehrer, bildete Hummel jedoch viele Vertreter der ersten Pianistengeneration des 19. Jahrhunderts aus: Henselt, Hiller, Mendelssohn und Thalberg profitierten von Hummels Unterricht. Andere Pianisten jeder Zeit wurden ebenfalls von Hummel beeinflusst. Schumann überlegte, bei ihm Unterricht zu nehmen (tat es jedoch nicht), doch beschäftigte er sich mit Hummels Verzierungen für die rechte Hand, wie die *Abegg-Variationen* op. 1 und andere Frühwerke belegen. Auch Liszt kam mit Hummels Musik in Berührung, indem er als junger Klaviervirtuose und Konzertreisender dessen Klavierkonzerte op. 85 und 89 spielte. Selbst Chopin muss Hummels Werke gekannt haben, da einige seiner frühen Stücke stilistische, teilweise sogar melodische Ähnlichkeiten aufweisen. Eine von Hummels herausragenden Leistungen ist seine Klavierschule von 1828, ein über 450 Seiten starkes Werk, das den Anspruch hat, den Schüler „vom ersten Unterricht an bis zur vollständigsten Ausbildung"[1] zu begleiten. Es erschien bei Tobias

Haslinger (s. Stück Nr. 10 dieser Anthologie) in Wien und ist wahrscheinlich die erste umfassende Klavierschule des 19. Jahrhunderts, in der die technischen Konzepte enthalten sind, die als Grundlagen für das virtuose Klavierspiel jenes Jahrhunderts dienten.

Abgesehen von Hummels gründlicher Unterrichtsmethode zeichnet sich die Klavierschule vor allem durch Hummels pädagogische Erkenntnisse und Betrachtungsweisen aus: Interaktion zwischen Schüler und Lehrer, Motivation sowie die Gestaltung einer Unterrichtsstunde sind einige der Themen, mit denen sich Hummel befasste.

August Eberhard Müller (1767–1817)

Müller war allem Anschein nach ein Lehrer, Musiker und Komponist, dessen Werk zu seinen Lebzeiten hohes Ansehen genoss. Als ausgebildeter Pianist, Organist und Flötist wurde Müller 1800 Adjunkt und 1804 Nachfolger von J.A. Hiller als Kantor der Thomaskirche in Leipzig, ein Amt, das vorher u.a. J.S. Bach innehatte. 1810 wurde er zum Kapellmeister in Weimar ernannt. Müller komponierte Unterrichtsstücke sowohl für Flöte als auch für Klavier, letztere mit beachtlichem Erfolg. Obwohl seine *Pianoforteschule* von 1804 eine aktualisierte und erweiterte Ausgabe der *Pianoforteschule* von Löhlein war, wird ihr Erfolg durch die Tatsache verdeutlicht, dass Carl Czerny 1825 die Neuausgabe von Müllers Klavierschule begleitete und der Pariser Klaviervirtuose Friedrich Kalkbrenner Müllers Werk als Vorlage für sein eigenes Klavierlehrbuch verwendete.

Wie nicht anders zu erwarten, waren einzelne Stücke von Müller im gesamten 19. Jahrhundert erhältlich. Als Musiker spielte Müller zahlreiche zeitgenössische Werke (z.B. 1801 Haydns *Schöpfung*), und als Gelehrter schrieb er über die Spielpraxis in Mozarts Klavierkonzerten (1797).

Leopold Mozart (1719–1787)

Obwohl er heute hauptsächlich als Vater von W.A. Mozart bekannt ist, war Leopold Mozart ebenfalls ein bedeutender Musiker, Komponist und Pädagoge. Nachdem er zunächst Philosophie studierte, wurden ihm seine musikalischen Aktivitäten immer wichtiger. Über einen Zeitraum von 20 Jahren stieg er vom vierten Violinisten zum Vizekapellmeister im Hoforchester des Erzbischofs Leopold Freiherr von Firmian in Salzburg auf. Darüber hinaus gab er Geigen- und Klavierunterricht und veröffentlichte 1756 seine hoch angesehene *Violinschule*. Mozarts Fähigkeit, effektive Unterrichtsstücke zu schreiben, ist in den Notenbüchern für seine zwei Kinder, Nannerl und Wolfgang Amadeus, belegt. Seine Kompositionen umfassen zahlreiche Sinfonien, Serenaden, Konzerte und Klavierstücke, obwohl viele Werke als verschollen gelten. Von den noch existierenden Stücken werden die Tänze und kürzeren Klavierstücke am häufigsten gespielt.

Wolfgang Amadeus Mozart (1756–1791)

Mozart wurde in eine äußerst musikalische Familie hineingeboren. Sein Vater Leopold war Orchesterviolinist und Lehrer in Salzburg, und seine ältere Schwester Nannerl hatte bereits ihre Fähigkeiten als Pianistin unter Beweis gestellt. Mozart machte im Musikunterricht rasche Fortschritte – so rasch, dass sein Vater ihn zu einer Konzertreise durch Deutschland und anschließend nach London und Paris mitnahm, die dreieinhalb Jahre dauerte. Danach ließ sich Mozart 1766 in Salzburg nieder. Von 1769–1772 folgten alljährliche Reisen nach Italien, auf denen Mozart – wie in seinem gesamten Leben – Kontakt zu vielen anderen Musikern

---

[1] Hummel, J. N., *Anweisung zum Piano-forte spielen* (Wien: Haslinger, 1828)

knüpfte. Anfang der 1780er-Jahre schien Mozart sich in ein Leben als freischaffender Musiker in all seiner Vielfalt eingefunden zu haben. Einige seiner erfolgreichsten Klavierkonzerte stammen aus dieser Zeit, ebenso viele Streichquartette, von denen er einige an der Seite ihres Widmungsträgers, Joseph Haydn, spielte. Am Ende des Jahrzehnts (und zu Beginn des nächsten) feierte Mozart mit Werken wie *Cosi fan tutte* und *Die Zauberflöte* große Erfolge als Opernkomponist.

Die verschiedenen Lebensabschnitte des Komponisten spiegeln sich in der Vielseitigkeit seiner Klavierkompositionen wider. Einige seiner frühesten Werke entstanden, als Mozart erst fünf Jahre alt war, eine Zeit, in der er hauptsächlich kürzere Tänze schrieb. Zu seinen Werken als Erwachsener zählen Sonaten, Variationen und Einzelstücke – viele davon waren für den Eigengebrauch geschrieben.

Franz Schubert (1797–1828)

Schuberts wurde zunächst von seinem Vater und seinen Brüdern unterrichtet, die ihm Klavier, Violine und Viola beibrachten. Im Alter von elf Jahren erhielt er ein Chorstipendium, das ihm eine Ausbildung bei Salieri ermöglichte. Mit 16 Jahren entschied sich Schubert für eine Ausbildung als Lehrer und begann ein Jahr später, in der Schule seines Vaters zu arbeiten. Mit 17 schrieb er bereits einige seiner frühen Meisterwerke für Klavier und Gesang, den *Erlkönig* und *Gretchen am Spinnrade*. 1816 gab Schubert seinen Lehrerposten auf und ging nach Wien, wo er im Stadtzentrum lebte und sich auf das Komponieren konzentrierte. Eine Zeit der finanziellen Unsicherheit folgte, bis er Ende 1819 sein erstes größeres Kammermusikstück, das *Forellenquintett*, schrieb. Im Frühjahr 1821 führte der Erfolg des *Erlkönigs* zur Veröffentlichung seiner Lieder durch Diabelli, was ihm eine kurze Zeit der finanziellen Sicherheit einbrachte. Von 1820–23 beschäftigte er sich vorwiegend mit der Komposition von Opernmusik, einem nicht besonders erfolgreichen Unterfangen. In seinen drei letzten Lebensjahren widmete er sich der Komposition von Kammermusik und sinfonischen Werken.

Mit wenigen Ausnahmen legte Schubert in seinen Klavierkompositionen nicht so viel Wert auf die äußerlichen technischen Aspekte, die einige seiner Zeitgenossen anwandten. Stattdessen liegen die Herausforderungen seiner Stücke immer in der Musik selbst und dem Bevorzugen von musikalischer Aussage zu rein technischer Darstellung.

Daniel Steibelt (1765–1823)

Steibelts Leben spiegelt zum Großteil die Umstände wider, unter denen viele Musiker und Komponisten damals lebten. Wie Häßler und Field lebte und arbeitete Steibelt nicht in seinem Geburtsland, sondern in verschiedenen anderen Ländern und ließ sich schließlich in Russland nieder. Vielleicht machten Steibelts Persönlichkeit und Geschäftsbeziehungen die relativ regelmäßigen Ortswechsel erforderlich. Zeitgenössischen Berichten zufolge war er eitel und extravagant und hatte zudem einen Hang zum Betrug. Unbezahlte Schulden und Vertragsbrüche sowie seine Neigung, leicht veränderte Werke (meist seine eigenen) als neue Kompositionen zu verkaufen, brachten Steibelt einen zweifelhaften Ruf ein. Es ist zwar unbestritten, dass er gut Klavier spielen konnte, doch bediente er als Komponist mit seinen Werken hauptsächlich den damals gerade aktuellen Musikgeschmack. Steibelts beste Kompositionen findet man im Genre des kurzen Charakterstücks für Klavier – ob Etüde oder Präludium. Da sich der musikalische

Inhalt größtenteils durch Erfindungsgeist auszeichnet und in einem relativ kurzen Format präsentiert wird, sind Steibelts Miniaturen oft ungewöhnlich effektiv. Von besonderer Bedeutung für Klavierschüler und Lehrer sind u.a. sein Klavierlehrbuch *Methode* (1805) sowie die *50 Etüden* op. 78.

Johann Baptist Vanhal (1739–1813)

Der böhmische Komponist Vanhal erhielt eine Ausbildung als Sänger und Geiger (später auch als Pianist), bevor er mit 21 Jahren nach Wien ging. Dort arbeitete er als Privatlehrer und unterrichtete u.a. den jungen Ignaz Pleyel. 1769 begab er sich auf eine zweijährige Konzertreise durch Italien, bevor er nach Wien zurückkehrte. Als Komponist schien er zu bestimmten Zeiten in verschiedenen Genres zu arbeiten. 1780 wandte er sich von den Sinfonien ab und hörte einige Jahre später auf, Streichquartette zu komponieren. Stattdessen konzentrierte er sich auf Klavier- und Kirchenmusik. Die zahlreichen Veröffentlichungen seiner Werke zu seinen Lebzeiten machen Vanhal zu einer bedeutenden Persönlichkeit des Musiklebens, obgleich einige seiner Werke nur als Manuskript existieren. Daher kann es gut sein, dass ein umfassender Überblick über seine Leistungen noch aussteht.

Carl Maria von Weber (1786–1826)

Webers frühe Jahre sind typisch für viele Musiker seiner Zeit. Er erhielt seinen ersten Musikunterricht von seinem Vater und mehreren anderen Musikern. Durch seine Reisen durch Deutschland und Österreich kam Weber in Kontakt mit Michael Haydn (Joseph Haydns Bruder und selbst ein viel beachteter Komponist) sowie dem Komponisten und Musiktheoretiker Georg Joseph Vogler, der Weber den konsequenten Unterricht erteilte, den dieser brauchte. Bis 1810 zog Weber häufig um und übte eine Reihe von musikalischen und teilweise auch Verwaltungstätigkeiten aus. Ein Gerichtsverfahren gegen Weber und seinen Vater, im Zuge dessen beide verhaftet wurden und schließlich Württemberg verlassen mussten, hatte tiefgreifende Auswirkungen auf Weber. Entschlossen, sein Leben zu ändern, verbrachte er die nächsten zwei Jahre damit zu komponieren, Konzerte zu geben und nicht über seine Verhältnisse zu leben. Schon bald folgte eine Ernennung zum Hof- und/oder Theaterdirigenten, von 1813 bis 1816 in Prag und von 1817 bis 1821 in Dresden. In dieser Zeit unternahm er außerdem Konzertreisen. Für die wohl bedeutendste Veränderung in Webers Leben war die große Beliebtheit seiner Oper *Der Freischütz* (1820) verantwortlich, ein Werk, das ihm sowohl in Deutschland als auch international Erfolg einbrachte.

Webers Klavierstücke sind zwar sehr charakteristisch, jedoch schwer zu beschreiben. Sie sind eindeutig melodieorientiert wie viele von Webers mehrstimmigen Kompositionen. Ein besonderer Schwerpunkt liegt auf Tanzformen und punktierten Rhythmen, die seinen Musikstil unterstreichen. Als Pianist bevorzugte Weber raffinierte und oft virtuose Passagen für die rechte Hand, schnelle Akkordfolgen, Überkreuzen der Hände und Sprünge, die weit über eine Fünf-Finger-Position hinausgehen. In diesem Sinne beruhen Webers Klavierkompositionen auf der fließenden Tonleiter- und Arpeggiotechnik, die Hummel bevorzugte, nehmen jedoch eine Mittelstellung zwischen Hummel und dem von Chopin und Liszt geforderten Klavierspiel ab 1830 ein.

CD Track List / Plages du CD / CD-Titelverzeichnis

No.	Title	Composer	Duration
1.	Minuet in D Minor	Leopold Mozart	1:12
2.	Minuet in F Major	Leopold Mozart	0:43
3.	Minuet KV6/IIIa	Wolfgang Amadeus Mozart	0:53
4.	Piano piece Op. 125 No. 7	Anton Diabelli	0:34
5.	Piano piece Op. 125 No. 6	Anton Diabelli	0:41
6.	Minuet KV1e	Wolfgang Amadeus Mozart	0:50
7.	Minuet in C Major	Leopold Mozart	0:59
8.	Deutscher Tanz Hob. IX:8	Joseph Haydn	0:39
9.	Ecossaise Op. 52 No. 5	Johann Nepomuk Hummel	0:39
10.	Sonatina in C Major	Tobias Haslinger	1:09
11.	Deutscher Tanz WoO 42 No. 1	Ludwig van Beethoven	0:42
12.	Ecossaise WoO 86	Ludwig van Beethoven	0:32
13.	Allegro KV3	Wolfgang Amadeus Mozart	1:12
14.	Minuet KV5	Wolfgang Amadeus Mozart	1:21
15.	Deutscher Tanz Hob.IX:12 No. 1	Joseph Haydn	0:36
16.	Minuet KV2	Wolfgang Amadeus Mozart	1:07
17.	Sonatina Op. 41 No. 1	Johann Baptist Vanhal	1:45
18.	Bourée in E Minor	Leopold Mozart	1:02
19.	Allegretto in C Major	Johann Baptist Cramer	0:40
20.	Allemande Op. 4 No. 9	Carl Maria von Weber	0:41
21.	Allemande Op. 4 No. 2	Carl Maria von Weber	0:39
22.	Kontretanz Hob. XXXIc:17b	Joseph Haydn	0:41
23.	Ecossaise in G Major	Johann Wilhelm Hässler	0:37
24.	Cantabile in A Minor	Daniel Steibelt	0:58
25.	Praeludium & Air Russe	Johann Baptist Cramer	1:28
26.	Un poco adagio (Air Russe)	Johann Nepomuk Hummel	0:33
27.	Siciliano in G Minor	August Eberhard Mueller	2:06
28.	Ecossaise WoO 23	Ludwig van Beethoven	0:48
29.	Ecossaise D. 145 No. 4	Franz Schubert	0:32
30.	Deutscher Tanz D. 972 No. 3	Franz Schubert	0:40

Total duration   **27:00**